T0341986

The Sacred Psyche

Marie-Louise von Franz, Honorary Patron

**Studies in Jungian Psychology
by Jungian Analysts**

Daryl Sharp, General Editor

THE SACRED PSYCHE

A Psychological Approach
to the Psalms

EDWARD F. EDINGER

Transcribed and Edited by Joan Dexter Blackmer

To those individuals who carry the torch of
consciousness through times of trouble.

National Library of Canada Cataloguing in Publication Data

Edinger, Edward F. (Edward Ferdinand),
  The sacred psyche: a psychological approach to the psalms /
  Edward F. Edinger; edited by Joan D. Blackmer.

(Studies in Jungian psychology by Jungian analysts; 108)

Includes bibliographical references and index.

ISBN 9781894574099

1. Bible. O.T. Psalms-Psychology.
2. Jungian Psychology-Religious aspects-Christianity.
I. Blackmer, Joan Dexter. II. Title. III. Series.

BS1430.5.E35 2004   223'.2'0019   C2003-902433-4

Copyright © 2004 by Dianne C. Cordic
All rights reserved.

INNER CITY BOOKS
21 Milroy Crescent Toronto, ON M1C 4B6, Canada
416-927-0355
www.innercitybooks.net / sales@innercitybooks.net

Honorary Patron: Marie-Louise von Franz.
Publisher and General Editor: Daryl Sharp.
Senior Editor: Victoria Cowan.

INNER CITY BOOKS was founded in 1980 to promote the
understanding and practical application of the work of C.G. Jung.

Cover: David playing a psaltery. From Hours of Bonaparte Ghislieri.
  (MS Yates Thompson 29, fl04v; British Library, London)

Printed and bound in Canada by Rapido Livres Books
Reprinted 2024

CONTENTS

See page 159 for other titles by Edward F. Edinger

I am not . . . addressing myself to the happy possessors of faith, but to those many people for whom the light has gone out, the mystery has faded, and God is dead. For most of them there is no going back, and one does not know either whether going back is always the better way. To gain an understanding of religious matters, probably all that is left us today is the psychological approach. That is why I take these thought-forms that have become historically fixed, try to melt them down again and pour them into moulds of immediate experience.

—C.G. Jung, "Psychology and Religion," CW 11, par. 148.

[We] . . . should bend to the great task of reinterpreting all the Christian traditions. . . . [And since] it is a question of truths which are anchored deep in the soul . . . the solution of this task must be possible.

—C.G. Jung, "Answer to Job," CW 11, par. 754.

Illustrations

Frontispiece. David Playing a Psaltery.
(From a drawing in pen and ink and purple wash on parchment,
by Fra Angelico; British Museum;
in Ronald Knox, *The Psalms in Latin and English)*

Editor's Foreword

In "Answer to Job," Jung urges those who can to "bend to the great task of reinterpreting all the Christian traditions."[1] For many years, Edinger dedicated a goodly portion of his creative energy to that "great task." *The Sacred Psyche* is the seventh and last volume in his effort to fulfill the assignment he had accepted—and the number seven is of great psychological significance.[2] At his death in July 1998, he had taken this work as far as he could. Although he would be the first to say his was only a start, he has laid the groundwork for others to build on.

Originally, Edinger envisioned *The Sacred Psyche* as an amply illustrated book discussing all 150 Psalms. For the lectures presented in this book, he narrowed that down to fifteen. Eight months before he died, Edinger and I spoke of the importance of putting those lectures into book form and he again briefly considered including all the Psalms. But his energy was spent. After his death, I knew that his work on the Psalms must be published, so with the support of Daryl Sharp and Dianne Cordic, Edinger's partner, I took up the task.

Edinger presented this material in differing ways in at least two seminars, one in the spring of 1983 at the Jung Institute in San Francisco, one in October 1984 at the Centerpoint Conference in Nashua, New Hampshire. Thanks to the generosity of Dianne Cordic, I have had the use of his concise handwritten notes for the lectures, with their many textual amplifications. These made his intentions clearer to me than might otherwise have been the case and enabled me to weave the versions together into a coherent whole.

While the rest of us see dimly through foggy glasses, Edinger's vision is clear, precise, eloquently presented. In his remarks on Psalm 1 he gives us the etymology of the word *torah:* "to throw out a finger and point the way." When lecturing, he often uses the phrase, "you see . . ." Wherever possible, I have kept that phrase in the text—he is pointing the way for the rest of us, helping us to see what he sees so clearly.

Edinger knew keenly the appropriate place of the ego when exploring the mysteries of the Self. As Jung says, "Because of his little-ness . . . [man] must, in order to survive, always be mindful of his im-potence."[3] With this in mind, much as Jung used a personal, feeling voice in "Answer to Job," I have kept, whenever I could, Edinger's own informal language.

My thanks go to the Detloff Library in San Francisco, and to Cen-terpoint, now in St. Louis, for copies of the tapes from which I tran-scribed Edinger's spoken words. My thanks also to Peggy Sugars who, with others, originally transcribed the San Francisco version.

Edinger's work is of vital importance to many people. Among them are four to whom this book owes a great deal. Mary Lyn Ray, with her gift of language and her deep experience of the psyche, has been a steady and invaluable overseer of the project. Karen Thorkil-sen not only solved many technical puzzles for me but also, with sen-sitivity and comprehension, contributed greatly with her editorial eye. In addition, without the warm support of Dianne Cordic and Daryl Sharp, this book could not have come into being.

My greatest debt is to Edinger himself: teacher, colleague, friend. I first met him in 1984 at the Centerpoint Conference. I was stunned then by his presence and by the depth and clarity of his work, an im-pression that has only grown stronger in the ensuing years. Now, as I read his commentary on Psalm 1, "The Blessed Man," I feel the wholeness he speaks of there also describes his own life. He was, in-deed, "consciously and appropriately related to the Self."

In *The Sacred Psyche,* Edinger speaks of his work as a translation from the traditional Judeo-Christian context to a modern psychologi-cal one. The original preface to the King James translation of the Bi-ble, published in 1611, contains these lines:

> Translation it is that openeth the window, to let in the light; that breaketh the shell, that we may eat the kernel; that putteth aside the curtain, that we may look into the most Holy place; that removeth the cover of the well, that we may come by the water.[4]

This is what Edinger has given us—the opportunity to drink living water.

Introduction

In *Mysterium Coniunctionis* Jung writes:

> Any renewal not deeply rooted in the best spiritual tradition is ephemeral;
> but the dominant that grows from historical roots acts like a living being
> within the ego-bound man. He does not possess it, it possesses him.[5]

Jung tells us here that every individual psychological development with any depth to it—not just an ephemeral tadpole in the puddle of life—must be connected to "the best spiritual tradition." Certainly the best spiritual tradition of the Western psyche is based on the Judeo-Christian Scriptures. That means, then, that we are obliged to assimilate this great archetypal treasury to the new psychological *Weltanschauung*. We dare not remain disconnected. We must reinterpret it in terms of our modern knowledge of depth psychology, and it is this purpose that lies behind my study of the Psalms.

Joseph Henderson has recalled Jung saying in a private conversation that he read the Bible not for its religious content but for its marvelous psychological content. That's what I have in mind here.

The Psalms occupy a unique position in the Bible. On the one hand, they contain the distilled essence of the Hebrew Scriptures; on the other hand, they prefigure the image of Christ and provide a bridge to the drama of the Christian Passion. I think it could be said that if we lost the narratives of the Crucifixion they could be reconstructed by an imaginative elaboration of the Psalms, especially Psalm 22. The more I study the Psalms, the more impressed I am with the fact that the image of Christ is embedded in them.

The Psalms are the prayer book of both the Jews and the Christians, and as the Psalms themselves tell us, Yahweh dwells within them. Psalm 22:3, referring to Yahweh, says: "Thou art holy, O thou that inhabitest the praises of Israel"—and the Psalms are a book of praises. Psychologically, this means that these texts embody the living presence of the Self.

Yahweh inhabits the Psalms because, clearly, they were written out

11

of multiple encounters with the *numinosum*.[6] Therefore they have the power to constellate the archetype of the God-image in those individuals who are open and receptive to their influence. They can lead one toward the experience which generated them. I've discovered, in fact, that one appreciates the Psalms most when dealing personally with the same psychic depths they record—and it may very well take a psychic crisis to experience their value. I have known several quite irreligious people who were astonished to discover that certain Psalms were the only thing that spoke to their condition during a period of grave psychic upheaval. They found companionship there, evidence that someone had been in the same place before them—and the value of such companionship should not be underestimated.

I must tell you that the Psalms are the heaviest material I have ever dealt with psychologically. I've worked on classical mythology, alchemy, the Old Testament and the New Testament. But none of these has had the weight that I've felt working on the Psalms. Sometimes, after dealing only briefly with one image, I would be utterly exhausted. It was as though I had been lifting huge boulders—that was the image that came to me. And in fact I think something of that sort is what happens. That's what we do when we work psychologically on this kind of deep material. We attempt to pry these great psychic megaliths, these huge stones, out of their religious context in order to make them available for direct experience. But this effort does involve moving great weights and it's no easy task. I offer these remarks so you can be on the alert to see for yourself whether you experience a similar fatigue.

One might say that the archetypal images, so relevant to the individual Western psyche, have been built like great slabs into the vast edifice of traditional Judeo-Christianity, into the whole dogmatic, liturgical and ecclesiastical structure. A collective edifice of immense proportions, it has housed the Western psyche for two thousand years or more. But it is in the process of collapsing. It is falling into ruins. The precious stones that have gone to make it up must now be rescued and built into a new structure, much as the stones of the pagan Roman temples were quarried in order to build Christian temples.

There is a difference of scholarly opinion concerning the dates and authorship of the Psalms. By all objective criteria, they are an anthology written over several centuries by various authors. Nonetheless, tradition assigns the authorship of the entire Psalter to David. And certainly the book is a unified work breathing the same numinous spirit throughout. Thus, from the psychological viewpoint, we can consider the traditional single-authorship of David to express, if not a literal fact, certainly a psychological one.

Figure 1. David Composing the Psalms.
(The Canterbury Psalter; British Library Board)

The designation "Psalms" is derived from the New Testament and has its origin in the Greek translation of the Old Testament—the Septuagint—where, in one codex, the Book of Psalms is called "Psalmoi." In another codex it's called the "Psalterion," referring to the harp-like instrument called a psalter or psalterion, which was used to accompany the singing of the Psalms.

The Hebrew name for the Psalms is *Tehillim,* meaning hymns or praises. And that term derives from the word *tehillah* which means to praise. So the Psalms are a book of praises, and that theme becomes particularly evident in the final Psalms where nothing but praise is mentioned. I'll speak more about that when we talk about Psalm 150.

We have several images that come together here. First, we have the basic idea of praise—praise to Yahweh. That the Psalms were sung carries the feeling of poetry and the power of constellating the unconscious in the way poetry does. And then there is music: as the psalterion is plucked during the singing of the words, so too are the strings of the soul.

As far as the traditional appreciation of the Psalms is concerned, I don't think a much better one can be found than the one given by Luther. It was he, you know, who translated the Hebrew Scriptures into German. Listen to what he says in his second preface to the German Psalter. This was written in 1528 and there's something quite remarkable in it:

> There you look into the hearts of all the saints as into a beautiful gay garden, indeed as into heaven; and in that garden you see spring up lovely, bright, charming flowers, flowers of all sorts of beautiful and joyous thoughts about God and His mercy. Again, where do you find words expressing sorrow more deeply and picturing its misery and wretchedness more tellingly than the words that are contained in the Psalms of lament? Here you look once more into the hearts of all the saints as into death, indeed as into hell; how dark and gloomy is it there, because of the grievous spectacle of the wrath of God which has to be faced in so many ways! Again, wherever they speak of fear or hope, they use such words that no painter could portray either fear or hope with equal force and no Cicero or orator could fashion them in like manner. And the very best thing is that

they speak such words about God and to God. . . .

This explains, moreover, why the Psalter is the favorite book of all the saints, and why each one of them, whatever his circumstances may be, finds in it Psalms and words which are appropriate to the circumstances in which he finds himself and meet his needs as adequately as if they were composed exclusively for his sake, and in such a way that he himself could not improve on them nor could he find or desire any better Psalms or words. . . .

To sum up: if you want to see the holy Christian Church painted in glowing colours, and in a form which is really alive, and if you want this to be done in a miniature, you must get hold of the Psalter, and there you will have in your possession a fine, clear, pure mirror which will show you what Christianity really is;

And here's the interesting thing to me:

yea, you will find yourself in it and the true *"gnothi seauton"* ("know thyself"), and God himself and all his creatures, too.[7]

I was startled to find Luther striking this modern psychological note.

Well, I read that because it's part of our "best spiritual tradition," written in 1528. But it is one-sided and I must try to balance it because although it's a beautiful and profound appreciation of the Psalms, it is an old-fashioned attitude. To balance it, I must mention some of my own past attitudes and reactions.

The Psalms have always been difficult for me. I haven't liked them. They have a kind of pushy piety that rubs me the wrong way. And I don't think I'm alone in that reaction because I believe modern Western culture has had rather enough of ostentatious religiosity. Our religious wars, our inquisitions, our self-righteous preachers of religious certainty—they all have generated a healthy skepticism concerning facile talk about God. When I'm in that mood, cool Greek reason once more has considerable appeal. This is what makes Augustine's *Confessions* so uncomfortable to me and, I think, to a lot of people. He puts us off by his easy familiarity with God and also by a kind of sycophancy to the Deity. How refreshing it is, by comparison, to read Jung's "Answer to Job."

My view is that we must be true to our modern Western reality and to the empirical standpoint that has created psychology. At the same time, we must do our very best to integrate material that derives from the traditional sources. The fact is that there is a sacred dimension to the psyche. Deity does exist. The sacred psyche is an empirical reality, and we must seek it in its natural habitat—where it lives. The Psalms themselves tell us that Yahweh inhabits the praises of Israel (22:3), and so we must study the Psalms.

One stumbling block in the Psalms is the rough, almost primitive nature of the relation to God they express. They have an archaic quality. That roughness, that uncouthness, is very uncomfortable for rational levels of consciousness. Yet, it is this very archaic quality that transmits the power and the depth of the Psalms. Experience teaches us that the *numinosum* is encountered in the archaic levels of the psyche. It is not something pretty and finely differentiated, not the god of the philosophers. It is a whole different thing—"barbaric, infantile, and abysmally unscientific," as Jung acknowledges in a letter to Erich Neumann.[8]

That level of the psyche can be found in all of us—provided one is able to penetrate deeply enough—and it is from just that level that the *numinosum* emerges. The more deeply one goes into the material, the more the feeling of distaste I mentioned earlier dissipates. At the basic level, one profound experience deepens another.

There is a wonderful Jewish legend about the function of the Psalms. The more contact I have with these legends the more impressed I am with their psychological wisdom. They supplement all the Biblical accounts with an accumulation of exceedingly rich lore. It is as though the collective psyche, in order to enlarge the implications of the traditional Biblical material, has woven all this lore to amplify the initial images much the way one amplifies a dream image. Here is an example:

> When King David's workmen began to build the House of God, they dug the drain for the altar very deep and inadvertently lifted the shard on the Mouth of the Abyss. Instantly the Waters of the Deep began to rise to

flood the earth. David knew that unless the Mouth of the Abyss were sealed again, the world would be destroyed. He also knew that only a stone with the Ineffable Name upon it could seal the Abyss. . . .

David lowered the stone with the Holy Name on it sixteen thousand ells, and tightly sealed the Mouth of the Abyss. But it was soon discovered that the earth below had lost its moisture and even the rains were not enough to grow the crops. King David then composed fifteen Psalms, and as each Psalm was completed, the Waters of the Deep rose one thousand ells. When the Waters reached within a thousand ells of the surface of the earth, he offered thanks to God, Who keeps the ground always moist enough for the crops, and does not allow the Abyss to sink one iota below, or rise one iota above, one thousand ells.[9]

I'm not going to try to interpret that. It is complete as it is.

Now a final note on the versions of the Psalms I will use. I think for English-speaking people, the Authorized King James Version must be the standard one because its venerable associations cause the archetypes to resound in a unique way for us. For full clarity of understanding, however, I think a modern version should also be used alongside the King James translation. The one I recommend is the Jerusalem Bible.

In addition, one really ought to have some kind of connection with the Hebrew original. Those fortunate enough to be able to read Hebrew may feel that archetypal resonance much more powerfully. I have practically no Hebrew at all. I just barely know the alphabet. But I do have an interlinear edition of the Psalms and with it I can locate and follow up certain Hebrew words that are especially significant. As you will see, I do that in Psalm 1 with the word "Torah," for instance, and it does add a whole other dimension.

The reason Jung puts so many Latin and Greek quotations into his works is because for many modern individuals the ancient languages constellate the archetypes. They have a mysterious quality not of the everyday. For that very reason granting them some attention amounts to pouring attention into the unconscious. It is an effort to pay homage to the historical levels of the psyche which are also the archetypal levels. With that in mind, I'll crawl my way through an interlinear Hebrew-English Psalter to locate certain words.

I should mention two other works that have been helpful to me in considering the Psalms. One is the three-volume work by C.H. Spurgeon entitled *The Treasury of David*. This is a vast anthology, a compilation of what has been said about individual Psalms and verses over a period of four or five centuries, and a wonderful aid to work with when you're examining some particular Psalm.

The other book I've found helpful and meaningful is Augustine's *Expositions on the Book of Psalms*. He wrote a large volume on all one hundred and fifty Psalms which is available in English translation. What's so remarkable about dealing with this kind of material is that the centuries just melt away because, essentially, Augustine is looking at the same text I'm looking at. He is commenting from his standpoint, and to be doing the same thing now on a much smaller scale— sixteen hundred years just melt away, and it is quite an experience. That is what happens when one deals with the fundamental texts. It is like looking at the stars in the sky. The constellations haven't changed, so that what the ancients saw, we see. And so it is with these basic Scriptures: what they saw, we see. It tends to generate a valuable sense of being rooted in the collective psyche.

There is one more small but important item I should mention before we turn to the Psalms themselves. The term "Lord," as used in the Authorized King James Version, is the translation for the Tetragrammaton, YHWH, which was thought too sacred to be pronounced. The Jerusalem Bible translates it as "Yahweh." So when LORD is capitalized here, that translates as Yahweh, while Lord refers to the ordinary meaning of the word as master.

Psalm 1
The Blessed Man

Beatus vir, qui non sequitur
Consilium impiorum,
Et viam peccatorum non ingreditur,
et in conventu protervorum non sedet;
Sed in lege Domini voluptas eius est,
et de lege eius meditatur die ac nocte.

Thus begins the Book of Psalms in the Vulgate translation, used throughout Western Christendom since the fourth century.[10]

It is immensely difficult to translate this material from one long-established context into a new empirical psychological context. I think the task is of the same magnitude as translating the symbolism of alchemy into psychological experience and understanding. Jung wrote four major volumes in his effort to do that: *Psychology and Alchemy, Alchemical Studies, Mysterium Coniunctionis* and *The Psychology of the Transference.* The sum total of all that work was to bring back into collective awareness a vast amount of symbolic material which had been lost to modern understanding.

Now it's not precisely the same situation with the Psalms, but there is a certain similarity. The Biblical material which has served as the basis for the traditional Western religious standpoint has lost its relevance for a significant percentage of modern people—something of the same situation as the alchemical material. And it's no easy task to make the shift.

What makes it doubly difficult is that the translation from the traditional context to a new psychological one can be understood and assimilated only if the reader brings to the effort a certain personal experience with the depths of the unconscious. If there is no such experience, it will be very difficult to understand the move from one realm to the other.

19

Nevertheless, I am going to make an initial effort to translate these fifteen Psalms into empirical psychological understanding. I don't feel I do a very good job—it's very hit or miss—and some Psalms receive more attention than others. My method is to treat them as though they were dreams. I don't know any other way to do it. So let's read the first "dream."

> 1. Blessed is the man that walketh not in the counsel of the ungodly, nor standeth in the way of sinners, nor sitteth in the seat of the scornful.
>
> 2. But his delight is in the law of the LORD; and in his law doth he meditate day and night.
>
> 3. And he shall be like a tree planted by the rivers of water, that bringeth forth his fruit in his season; his leaf also shall not wither; and whatsoever he doeth shall prosper.
>
> 4. The ungodly are not so; but are like the chaff which the wind driveth away.
>
> 5. Therefore the ungodly shall not stand in the judgment, nor sinners in the congregation of the righteous.
>
> 6. For the LORD knoweth the way of the righteous: but the way of the ungodly shall perish.[11]

I think it never fails—when I'm first presented with a dream, my reaction is "Oh my God, I haven't the faintest notion what that means!" So you go to work and you start with one image at a time; then, if grace helps out, some meaning starts to emerge.

The first word of the first verse of the Book of Psalms is *Beatus*—"blessed." And the whole Psalm describes the state of the blessed man. Now what does it mean psychologically to be blessed? If one follows up the different etymologies—Hebrew, Greek, Latin—and the usage in various places, what seems to emerge is that blessedness in the context of the Psalms is the goal of human existence and refers to being in a state of favor before God.

Well, that's certainly understandable psychologically. Blessedness would be the state of the ego when it's consciously and appropriately related to the Self. Some modern translations use the word "happy," but I don't believe blessedness is synonymous with happiness. Rather, I think it refers to being centered in one's wholeness, which includes the opposites. One commentator said that the blessed man was *"that one among a thousand who lives for the accomplishment of the end for which God created him."*[12] This, I think, would fit with the psychological implications of the term.

Taken as a whole, the Psalm contrasts two ways of being: the way of the righteous which leads to blessedness, and the way of the wicked or the ungodly. The two Hebrew terms are *tsaddik,* righteous or wise, and *rasha,* wicked. Unfortunately the word "righteous" has rather ambiguous connotations nowadays. Who among us does not think of "self-righteous" as soon as the word "righteous" comes up? But in its original sense it means "the straight, right way." Psychologically, we can think of the way of the righteous, *tsaddik,* as Self-oriented, whereas the way of the wicked, *rasha,* is antagonistic to the Self.

The text tells us that for the righteous, "his delight is in the law of the LORD; and in his law doth he meditate day and night." So the chief characteristic of the blessed man is that he strives to be obedient to the inner law. This then brings up a major symbolic image, not only for the Psalms but for the whole Hebrew Bible: the "law." The blessed man constantly relates to it, and this gives major importance to what is symbolized by the law.

The Hebrew word for law is *torah.* Its etymology is very interesting. I dig this all up out of the Old Testament word books and things like that, but it's not dead dusty work because living meaning emerges from following up these trails. And I can tell it's alive by the effect it has on me. Libido is released!

Torah. Everybody's heard that word, a very important term for the Jew. It derives from a verb, *yarah,* meaning "to throw, cast, direct, teach, instruct." The basic image behind this, as the books tell me, is to throw out the hand and finger, and point the right direction to go. Which way is it to Boston? You throw out your hand and point the way. That's the image and the experience at the root of the word *torah.*

Now one of the things that concerns me as I try to convey to you the material I've uncovered is that I'll tangle you up in too many different lines of thought simultaneously. You are all familiar with that phenomenon if you have dipped into Jung's *Mysterium Coniunctionis.* You don't have to go very far before feeling confused, lost. I constantly run the risk of doing the same thing with this material. On the other hand, if I don't take that risk, you won't have an opportunity to observe my psychological method.

So here is another of these beautiful Jewish legends. This comes from the Talmud and it talks about the Torah. For the believing Jew, especially the ancient Jew, *torah* had a very clear-cut meaning. It wasn't this symbolic image that I'm talking about. It was, first of all, the Ten Commandments, the literal law that God communicated to Moses. Secondly, it was the five books of Moses, the Pentateuch. So they thought they knew what they were talking about when they talked about the law. However, in the realm of the legends, things get more complicated; the psyche comes into the picture and the stories become richer and more psychological.

This legend in the Talmud conveys a sense of how precious the Torah was to the pious Jew. Yahweh has just presented it to Moses on Mt. Sinai, but it has been lost—they can't find it.

In the hour when Moses descended from before the Holy One, blessed be He, Satan came and said before Him: "Master of the World! The Tora, where is she?" [Notice the feminine personification.] He said to him: "I gave her to the earth." Satan went to the earth and said to her: "The Tora, where is she?" She said to him: *"God understandeth her way, and He knoweth her place."* (Job 28:23) Thereupon he went to the Sea, but the Sea said to him: "She is not with me." He went to the Deep, but the Deep said to him: "She is not in me, as it is written, *The Deep saith, She is not in me, and the Sea saith, She is not with me.* (Job 28:14) *Perdition and Death say, We have heard a rumor thereof with our ears."* (Job 28:22)

Satan returned and said before the Holy One, blessed be He: "Master of the World! I searched in the whole earth and found her not." He said to him: "Go to the Son of Amram!" He went to Moses and said to him:

"The Tora which the Holy One, blessed be He, gave you, where is she?" He said to him: "Who am I that the Holy One, blessed be He, should give me the Tora?" The Holy One, blessed be He, said to Moses: "Moses! Are you a liar?" He said before Him: "Master of the World! You have a hidden treasure in which You delight every day. Can I claim this benefit for myself?" The Holy One, blessed be He, said to Moses: "Since you have belittled yourself, she will be called by your name, as it is written: *Remember the Tora of Moses My Servant.*" (Mal. 3:22)[13]

Well, that's a legend about Satan looking for the Torah, and Moses not daring to acknowledge he had it. I think it's evident that in the legend more is implied by the term "Torah" than just a set of commandments. It is a much richer, mysterious and more complex entity than that.

Now I'm following a line here and I hope I don't lose you. This legend quotes several verses from Job 28. If one is going to do a full dream interpretation one has to follow up all these threads, so we go to the passages in Job that the legend refers to:

There is a path which no fowl knoweth, and which the vulture's eye hath not seen.

But where shall wisdom be found? and where is the place of understanding? Man knoweth not the price thereof; neither is it found in the land of the living.
The depth saith, It is not in me: and the sea saith, It is not with me.
It cannot be gotten for gold, neither shall silver be weighed for the price thereof.

Destruction and death say, We have heard the fame thereof with our ears.
God understandeth the way thereof, and he knoweth the place thereof.
(Job 28:7, 12-15, 22-23)

This reference is to Wisdom, that feminine helpmate who was with Yahweh when he created the world.[14] In Latin she was called *Sapientia Dei,* the Wisdom of God; in Greek, Sophia. And the Talmud's reference to this passage in relation to the lost Torah establishes the symbolic equation: Torah equals Wisdom. We might have guessed that because the word "torah," like "wisdom," is feminine.

The Job passage also connects the Torah with the image of the "path" or the "way." It speaks about Wisdom as "the path which no fowl knoweth, and which the vulture's eye hath not seen." So by this line of associations we arrive at the idea that the Torah is a path, just as we did by the etymology that spoke about throwing out the hand and pointing a direction with a finger—and a direction implies a path.

I must go a little bit further, hoping I haven't lost you entirely. In *Mysterium Coniunctionis* Jung discusses an alchemical text which uses this same passage from Job to describe the Philosophers' Stone: "Therefore says Job 28:7: The bird hath not known the path, neither hath the eye of the vulture beheld it. For this stone belongeth only to the proven and elect of God."[15] So a Biblical quotation referring to the path of Wisdom or the law of God—the Torah—is grafted onto the alchemical image of the Philosophers' Stone.

As Jung has demonstrated, the alchemists didn't know what they were doing. In other words, the unconscious lived through them. Therefore it's the unconscious that makes the connection between the path which the vulture has not seen and the Philosophers' Stone. But from this sequence of associations we end up with a symbolic equation that Torah equals the Philosophers' Stone. We've traveled through the centuries and through a whole series of interrelated symbolic materials to locate that connection. But this is the way we have to go, because this is how the collective psyche manifests itself. We are not dealing with theories or abstract constructions. We are trying to trace the reality of the collective psyche as these various images unfold through the centuries and as they move from one symbolic tradition to another.

The image of the path or the way appears in other major religious traditions as well. I chose the one leading to alchemy, but we also know that Christ identified himself with the way when he said: "I am the way, the truth and the life." (John 14:6) And in Chinese wisdom, especially Taoism, the archetype of the way is expressed in the central concept of Tao.

These are all amplifications of the archetypal image that lies at the root of *torah*, "the law of the Lord" that the blessed man delights in and meditates on day and night. If it is such an important archetypal image it will show up in modern material—and of course it does. It comes up in modern dreams as images of roads, paths, stepping stones, indications of a pathway or a direction or some way of guidance—a way to go that the ego doesn't know about, that has a non-ego quality to it. When one has lost the way psychologically and doesn't know what to do, it is very moving indeed to receive a dream that reveals that there *is* a way, there *is* an inner direction—a path. For that person, a hand is thrown out and a finger points the way.

I remember a young man who was lost—he had nothing pointing the way, neither vocationally nor in a more general sense. The "torah" was lost, and he didn't know how to be "righteous" in the original sense. One day he came with a dream: he was in a garden that seemed to be randomly planted; it had no structure. But as he looked closely, he saw stones, multicolored stones, embedded in that garden. Then it dawned on him: "Those are stepping stones!" In other words, there was a path. I knew it at once—you can tell when the shivers go up and down your spine—you know at once that something central has been struck. He didn't know it at once, but he'd found his way! He went on to become a psychiatrist.

So the blessed one, the so-called righteous one, is the one who delights in the law—in the way—and who meditates on it day and night. Then the Psalm offers another analogy: we're told in verse 3 that such a blessed one "shall be like a tree planted by the rivers of water, that bringeth forth his fruit in his season; his leaf also shall not wither; and whatsoever he doeth shall prosper."

As I've said, I can only deal with this text in the same way I would deal with a dream. If a person brought me a dream like this I'd say, "That reminds me of Jung's dream!" and I'd look it up in *Memories, Dreams, Reflections.* Here is what I'd find:

Soon afterward, in the spring and early summer of 1914, I had a thrice-repeated dream that in the middle of summer an Arctic cold wave descended and froze the land to ice. . . .

In the third dream frightful cold had again descended from out of the cosmos. This dream, however, had an unexpected end. There stood a leaf-bearing tree, but without fruit (my tree of life, I thought), whose leaves had been transformed by the effects of the frost into sweet grapes full of healing juices. I plucked the grapes and gave them to a large, waiting crowd.[16]

Well, as far as I'm concerned, that dream connects Jung with the blessed man whose delight is the law of the Lord. I don't need any more connection than that. But that's just one association. There are a great many others—the archetype of the tree is exceedingly rich in symbolic associations. Jung has a lengthy essay in which he summarizes the commonest associations pertaining to a tree:

> . . . growth, life, unfolding of form in a physical and spiritual sense, development, growth from below upwards and from above downwards, the maternal aspect (protection, shade, shelter, nourishing fruits, source of life, solidity, permanence, firm-rootedness, but also being "rooted to the spot"), old age, personality, and finally death and rebirth.[17]

To this list we might also add the images of a world center, a world axis, a connection between above and below, the Self in profile as a developmental process.[18] All these associations can be applied to the psalmist's image of the tree of the blessed man.

The fact that the tree is planted by rivers of water calls to mind the two trees in the Garden of Eden. This association would suggest that the righteous man has regained a connection with the lost Paradise through his contact with the suprapersonal center of the Self.

In the apocryphal book of Ecclesiasticus, Wisdom describes herself as many kinds of trees and, especially pertinent to this image, as a tree planted by the water: "I was exalted like a cedar in Libanus, . . . and grew up as a plane tree by the water."[19]

Then we hear of other trees too. There's the World Tree, Yggdrasil, of Norse mythology. And a great inverted cosmic tree in the *Upanishads:* "There is that ancient tree, whose roots grow upward and whose branches grow downward—that indeed is called the Bright, that is called Brahman, that alone is called the Immortal. All worlds are contained in it, and no one goes beyond."[20] And again in the *Bhagavad-Gita:*

> There is a fig tree
> In ancient story,
> The giant Ashvattha,
> The everlasting,
> Rooted in heaven,
> Its branches earthward;
> Each of its leaves
> Is a song of the Vedas,
> And he who knows it
> Knows all the Vedas.[21]

The Sephirotic Tree of the Kabbalists is also pictured as an inverted tree. In contrast, the Philosophical Tree of the alchemists, which symbolizes the alchemical process of transformation, grows from below upward (Figure 2, next page).

All these associations are relevant to this particular image of the "tree planted by the rivers of water." So we can make the symbolic equations that this tree is the tree of Jung's dream; the tree of Yggdrasil; the tree of the *Upanishads,* of the *Bhagavad-Gita* and the Kabbalistic tree of the Sephiroth, all three growing from above downward—from the transpersonal dimension down to the personal dimension. It is the Philosophical Tree of the alchemists, Wisdom's tree and the Tree of Life with the four rivers flowing from it. It's all those things.

Now, if one is doing with this Psalm what the righteous man is supposed to be doing—"his delight is in the law of the LORD; and in his law doth he meditate day and night"—all these images would be the content of the meditations. The meditation is the tree, too. You see? I'm trying to give you some sense of what those meditations would be, but I have to be careful—if you go too deep everything becomes everything else and you lose your bearings. Meaning welleth over. There is such a thing as too much meaning and not enough earthly standpoint.

But this isn't the end of the Psalm. After talking about the nature of the blessed man, the righteous one, the psalmist goes on to say: "The ungodly are not so; but are like the chaff which the wind driveth

Figure 2. The Philosophical Tree, surrounded by symbols of the *opus*.
(From Mylius, *Philosophia reformata;* 1622)

away." So we've got something opposed to this tree and the blessed man. In contrast to the righteous, we have what's called the wicked or the ungodly, described as chaff—empty husks without central substance. As the Self-oriented one is fruitful, substantial, nourishing, so the Self-alienated one is empty, trivial and weightless.

Augustine's interpretation of this particular phrase is that "the chaff which the wind driveth away" refers to "pride, in that it puffeth him up."[22] According to another commentator quoted by Spurgeon, "wind" means "whirlwind" and "shows the vehement tempest of death which sweeps away the soul of the ungodly."[23] Of course, no sooner is the word "whirlwind" used than we think of Job 38:1: "Then the LORD answered Job out of the whirlwind."

Etymology is very helpful as we try to understand what is translated as "wicked." The Hebrew word is *rasha*. One way of approaching the meanings of these Hebrew words is to see how they were translated into Greek in the third century B.C. This gives us some idea of the usage of that time which we can't know, but those Greek translators of the third century B.C. could. They were there. In the early Greek translation, the Septuagint, we find the word *rasha* translated into Greek in three different ways: "godless or impious," "sinful" and "lawless." They are not exactly the same, but the underlying meaning seems to be lack of awareness of the Deity.

I think that what we have here is not a moral judgment but rather an objective description of two psychological states. In other words, the human race isn't divided into two categories, one representing the righteous and the other the wicked. That is too concrete a projection. Rather, these two categories represent two psychological states of being, each experienced by one individual at different times. There will be certain occasions where one can experience what is called by that ambiguous word, righteousness, and there will be other times when one's psychological state will feel more like "the chaff that the wind driveth away." No individual is permanently and perfectly in relation to the Self—that doesn't exist.

Verse 5 then tells us that these two conditions will be separated out at the judgment: "Therefore the ungodly shall not stand in the judgment, nor sinners in the congregation of the righteous." This passage is considered to refer to the Last Judgment, the eschatological and decisive encounter, in psychological terms, with the activated Self.[24]

But the term "congregation of the righteous" is something different. It's a fascinating image. Psychologically it might correspond to what Jung calls the *Ecclesia spiritualis*. I am well aware that I am open to the criticism of defining one unknown with another, so just what is the *Ecclesia spiritualis?* Jung speaks of it in *Mysterium Coniunctionis*.[25] He doesn't say what it is, but the materials he presents that speak of it give some indication of what is meant by the term. It is a spiritual church as opposed to a concrete congregation: an invisible grouping of individuals, scattered in both time and space, who have had the same deep experience of the autonomous spirit.

Finally comes the statement: "For the LORD knoweth the way of the righteous: but the way of the ungodly shall perish." I understand this to be an allusion to the mutual and reciprocal process of knowing and being known that operates between the ego and the Self.

This last verse of Psalm 1, "For the LORD knoweth the way of the righteous but the way of the ungodly shall perish" says in effect that being known or seen by the Self means to live, but not being known is to perish. In one Biblical passage, Jesus says to sinners: "I never knew you."[26] The ungodly who do not know God in turn are not known by him. In other words there's a reciprocal quality to the relationship. Without a conscious connection with the Self, which brings about that reciprocal knowing and being known, the ego cannot survive. Thus one definition for existence might be that the basis for life is being known by and knowing God—or in psychological terms, seeing and being seen by the Self.[27]

Psalm 2
Why Do the Heathen Rage?

1. Why do the heathen rage, and the people imagine a vain thing?

2. The kings of the earth set themselves, and the rulers take counsel together, against the LORD; and against his anointed, saying,

3. Let us break their bands asunder, and cast away their cords from us.

4. He that sitteth in the heavens shall laugh: the LORD shall have them in derision.

5. Then shall he speak unto them in his wrath, and vex them in his sore displeasure.

6. Yet have I set my king upon my holy hill of Zion.

7. I will declare the decree: the LORD hath said unto me, Thou art my Son; this day have I begotten thee.

8. Ask of me, and I shall give thee the heathen for thine inheritance, and the uttermost parts of the earth for thy possession.

9. Thou shalt break them with a rod of iron; thou shalt dash them in pieces like a potter's vessel.

10. Be wise now therefore, O ye kings: be instructed, ye judges of the earth.

11. Serve the LORD with fear, and rejoice with trembling.

12. Kiss the Son, lest he be angry, and ye perish from the way, when his wrath is kindled but a little. Blessed are all they that put their trust in him.

You know, it takes more than one reading to really get what's being said here. I'll talk about certain aspects, and if you read it over again later I think it will take on more meaning.

This is the first of the so-called Messianic Psalms—those thought to describe the Messiah. Originally, it was probably a coronation song used at the inauguration of a new king of Israel. Interpreted eschatologically, it is taken to refer to the future Messianic Kingdom which, in Christian terms, would arrive with the Second Coming of Christ. The early Christian Fathers interpreted this Psalm as referring to Christ. For the Jews, it would be associated with the Messiah-to-be.

In Messianic symbolism, without going into all the sources, there are two aspects of the Messiah: Messiah ben Joseph and Messiah ben David. Another way of putting it is that the Messiah is split and comes twice: the first coming (Messiah ben Joseph) is with persecution, humiliation and apparent defeat; the second coming (Messiah ben David) is in glory, victory, judgment and final fulfillment.[28] Psalm 2 is a Psalm of the second advent of the Messiah. On the other hand, Psalm 22—which we will get to later—is a Messianic Psalm concerning the first advent.

Psychologically, Psalm 2 describes the inauguration in the psyche of the inner authority, the transpersonal "king." The secular aspect of the ego (in Hebrew, *goyim*, translated as "gentiles," "heathen") cannot stand, initially, to be ruled by anything other than itself. But the Messiah has come and has subordinated the heathen king—the secular ego—to its authority. So the "heathen rage" against being subordinated; they rage against the coming of the Messiah.

Well, the raging of the heathen at the coming of the Self—that's a well-known phenomenon in analytic work, I can assure you, because the inner transpersonal authority so often interdicts certain desires of the ego. The ego can't have things the way it wants—it wants a "vain thing" in terms of verse 1. The early experiences of the Self, the superordinant authority within the psyche, are an offense to the ego. The willful ego, therefore, when it encounters such an experience, rages against being subordinated. I cannot overemphasize how common this experience is. It is everywhere—within oneself and without. You won't get through this day without seeing an example of it, either inside or outside, or both. For the ego it is an intolerable bondage whose bands and cords must be broken. "Let us break their bands asunder, and cast away their cords from us." That's what verse 3 says.

But as this Psalm makes clear, once the Messiah has come—which means, in psychological terms, when the Self has really been constellated (these events don't take place until that constellation, that activation, has occurred)—when it does in fact come, then the willful protestations of the ego will not prevail.

In verse 7 the newly anointed king announces the message that he has received from God: "The LORD hath said unto me, Thou art my Son; this day have I begotten thee." There is an interesting sidelight about this passage which is psychologically relevant. It became a major proof-text for the so-called Adoptionist Christology. According to this doctrine,

> Jesus is regarded as the man whom God has elected for his own, the one in whom the Deity or the Spirit of God dwelt, and who, after being tested, was adopted by God and endowed with full dominion.[29]

This adoption took place at the baptism of Jesus when the voice from heaven said: "This is my beloved Son, in whom I am well pleased." (Matt. 3:17) Certain commentators consider that remark to derive from Psalm 2:7: "Thou art my Son; this day have I begotten thee." In a nutshell, the idea of Adoptionist Christology was that, at the time of his baptism, the spirit descended on Jesus and lived out of him. Then, when it came to the Crucifixion, it left him again and he was on his own. This is just one of countless examples of how the Christian myth and its detailed elaboration are interwoven with images from the Psalms.

With our psychological insights we can now understand all these images as referring to experiences of the individual in the course of individuation. Although the Adoptionist Christology was fairly quickly declared heretical, from a psychological point of view, as with all heretical variants of profound mythological images, both the orthodox and the heretical views are true. But the Church can't survive with that viewpoint. The human psyche in its collective manifestation is factionalist to the core—individuals break up into factions and fight one another—and that's intolerable for the Church.

To survive in the world, the Church has first of all to be concerned with its integrity, its sufficient unity; therefore it cannot tolerate the side by side existence of paradoxical contraries. The individual, however, can and should. So Adoptionist Christology is just as true psychologically as is the orthodox view that God himself was incarnated in the womb of the Virgin Mary. It is part of the phenomenology of the Self which reconciles opposites and is beyond rational dichotomies.

Anyway, still speaking psychologically, as a result of this election experience of being adopted by the Self, the secular ego is then handed over to what we might call the "son" or the Self-oriented ego. This then leads to what the Psalm, in verse 8, speaks of as giving "thee the heathen for thine inheritance." I take that to mean that the libido, which had been in the hands of the secular heathen ego in the form of rage, is now made available to the Self-oriented ego. As that rage is assimilated, its energy becomes the inheritance of the Self-oriented ego, the "son."

For the secular ego, of course, it feels like a Last Judgment. Not only feels like it, it *is* a Last Judgment, because of what happens in verse 9: "Thou shalt break them with a rod of iron; thou shalt dash them in pieces like a potter's vessel." This same image is used in Revelation 2:27 to refer to the coming of the Apocalyptic Christ (Figure 3): "And he shall rule them with a rod of iron; as the vessels of a potter shall they be broken to shivers." The idea is that once the Self has been constellated and begets its "son"—its representative within the individual psyche—then the vessel of the heathen ego will be broken.

The image of the broken potter's vessel is depicted vividly in Jeremiah:

Then Yahweh said to Jeremiah, "Go and buy an earthenware jug. Take some of the elders of the people and some priests with you. Go out towards the Valley of Ben-hinnom, as far as the entry of the Gate of the Potsherds. There proclaim the words I shall speak to you. You are to say, 'Kings of Judah, citizens of Jerusalem! Listen to the word of Yahweh! Yahweh Sabaoth, the God of Israel, says this: . . . Because of this place, I mean to drain Judah and Jerusalem of sound advice; I will make them fall by the sword before their enemies, fall by the hand of people determined to kill them; I will give their corpses as food to the birds of heaven and the beasts of earth. And I will make this city a desolation, a derision; every passer-by will be appalled at it, and whistle in amazement at such calamity. I will make them eat the flesh of their own sons and daughters: they

Figure 3. The Apocalyptic Christ.
(From *The Complete Woodcuts of Albrecht Dürer*, fig. 107)

shall eat each other during the siege, in the shortage to which their enemies, in their determination to kill them, will reduce them."

"You are to break this jug in front of the men who are with you, and say to them, 'Yahweh Sabaoth says this: I am going to break this people and this city just as one breaks a potter's pot, irreparably.' "

(Jer. 19:1-11, Jerusalem Bible)

This is quite a big image, the deliberate breaking of a potter's vessel. It's an image of a psychosis! Images of small or unimportant broken plates and broken bowls are not uncommon in dreams and they mean that the particular containing attitude or viewpoint—a relationship perhaps—has broken. A new and presumably larger or more adequate container needs to be found for the contents. That can have auspicious implications; it can be a kind of death and rebirth if the individual is up to it. However, if in a dream a vessel of considerable import with sizable associations has been broken or is cracked, that's rather ominous.

The big psychological vessel for the individual is the ego, and the danger is that the ego will break under the impact of an assault from the unconscious. If that pot breaks, we have a psychosis. Psychologically, that is precisely what Jeremiah 19 is describing: Yahweh tells Jeremiah to show them an image of a psychosis. So we can think of Psalm 2, especially verse 9, as an indication of what can happen if the secular ego is not able to make the transition and cannot accept the coming of the Self-oriented ego, symbolized by the Messiah.

Yet breaking of the ego is an ambivalent thing. In the course of individuation the ego has to break to some extent in order for the larger standpoint of the Self to come into view. I don't think that experience can be completely avoided.[30] There's almost always a break of some kind.

The symbolism is analogous to the breaking of a bone. The break comes and then there is a period of relative confusion, helplessness and paralysis—just as there is with a broken bone. Afterward, if nature and circumstances are working properly, the bone heals, a callus forms at the site of the break and it is stronger than it was before. At that site it becomes almost unbreakable—if it mends. However, there are certain breaks which, if they are not tended to, become permanent and then there is no possibility of mending them.

Something like that also happens in the relationship of the ego to the Self. The Self breaks the ego's will. But, if the mending takes place, the ego is then knit together by a connection to the Self and is practically indestructible—because it has a transpersonal foundation. All this material derives from that statement in Psalm 2: "Ask of me, and I shall give thee the heathen for thine inheritance, . . . Thou shalt break them with a rod of iron; thou shalt dash them in pieces like a potter's vessel."

You see, here's how I understand the composition of the Psalms: they are the products of profound moments of religious inspiration—moments of intense personal experience on the part of the psalmist—in which the meaning of the experience welled out of the unconscious in relevant poetic images. It almost doesn't matter to us how the ego of the psalmist understood his Psalm. What we're interested in is the phenomenon itself, the creative expression of the unconscious which describes in this vivid imagery the nature of certain fundamental psychic experiences. And now that we have the psychological viewpoint, we can approach these fruits of profound personal experience and give them psychological references which were never before available.

Question from the audience having to do with the "adversarial phase" of the ego-Self relationship.

Edinger: I think it varies from one individual to another, but my impression is that those who are destined for maximum psychological development are apt to have particularly intense experiences of the adversarial phase. Jung gives us an example of that in *Memories, Dreams, Reflections,* where he talks about a dream concerning his visit to Africa.[31] It was the dream of the combat on the bridge with a Muslim prince. Jung was almost done in by that—he just barely overcame the prince. And he speaks of the aspect of the encounter with the Self in which the Self is the enemy of the ego. He interprets the Muslim prince as a kind of angelic being who attacked him because Jung had trespassed on his realm.

That happens when the ego presumes to go into the unconscious in order to understand it—to assimilate it to some extent—in terms of the ego's conscious categories of understanding. To the Self it is a trespass. And, as Jung says, angelic presences, those beings who belong to the archetypal psyche, don't know how things are in the conscious world; they need to be educated. Their initial hostility is really an indication of ignorance to some extent. But it is real hostility nonetheless, so it has to be dealt with. That is why the encounter with the unconscious requires a very canny and acute kind of attitude, not a naive and innocent one.

Psalm 8
What Is Man That Thou Art Mindful of Him?

1. LORD our Lord, how excellent is thy name in all the earth! who hast set thy glory above the heavens.

2. Out of the mouth of babes and sucklings hast thou ordained strength because of thine enemies, that thou mightest still the enemy and the avenger.

3. When I consider thy heavens, the work of thy fingers, the moon and the stars, which thou hast ordained;

4. What is man, that thou art mindful of him? and the son of man, that thou visitest him?

5. For thou hast made him a little lower than the angels, and hast crowned him with glory and honour.

6. Thou madest him to have dominion over the works of thy hands: thou has put all things under his feet:

7. All sheep and oxen, yea, and the beasts of the field;

8. The fowl of the air, and the fish of the sea, and whatsoever passeth through the paths of the seas.

9. O LORD our Lord, how excellent is thy name in all the earth!

Let's first consider the phrase in verse 2: "Out of the mouth of babes and sucklings hast thou ordained strength because of thine enemies."

It is interesting to follow how images of this sort are picked up in other traditional contexts and incorporated in analogous places. For instance, this passage is used in the Catholic liturgy for the feast day of the Massacre of the Holy Innocents. And Christ quotes it in Matthew 21:16. When children in the temple hailed him after his triumphal entry into Jerusalem, he said: "Yea; have ye never read, Out of the mouth of babes and sucklings thou hast perfected praise?"

Very interesting; it is the same text we have in Psalm 8, but with just a slight change, you see. Instead of "ordained strength" he says "perfected praise." And Christ mentions this same idea in another place, in Matthew 11:25. It shows that he's quite preoccupied with this image. There he says "I thank thee, O Father, Lord of heaven and earth, because thou hast hid these things from the wise and prudent, and hast revealed them unto babes."

Well, right away this brings up the archetype of the divine child. What distinguishes an image representing the archetype of the child from any old child? What's the difference? Is it proper to say of any child image in a dream, Ah, that's an example of the divine child? No. To be "divine" the child image must have something unusual or out of the ordinary about it. So if you have a dream of a child that is just born and can speak, for instance, that's the divine child. The divine child has something marvelous about it. In this Psalm we see something remarkable—God is strengthened out of the mouths of babes and sucklings! That's a marvel, and so it demonstrates that we're dealing with the archetype of the divine child.

Whenever this image comes up for me, I immediately think of the quotation that Jung so laboriously carved on the Bollingen stone (Figure 4). I don't know if any of you are stone carvers. I'm not, but my father was a cut-stone contractor. He had a mill that fabricated Indiana limestone, and as a youth I would often watch what went on in that mill. I can tell you it takes a long time, even with pneumatic instruments, to carve the lengthy inscription Jung carved on the Bollingen stone. And he didn't use pneumatic instruments. I've seen pictures. He used a hammer and chisel. That takes a long time! It demonstrates, then, the importance of what he chiseled so laboriously on that stone. He did it in Greek, and this is its translation:

> Time is a child—playing like a child—playing a board game—the kingdom of the child. This is Telesphoros, who roams through the dark regions of this cosmos and glows like a star out of the depths. He points the way to the gates of the sun and to the land of dreams.[32]

That's the divine child.

I want to give you another example of this same phenomenon from a totally different symbolic context. This is one way we assimilate these images psychologically—we see where they show up in dif-

'ο αιων παις εστι παιζων
πεττευων παιδος 'η βασιληιη
τελεσφορος διελαυνων τους
σκοτεινους του κοσμου τοπους
και 'ως αστηρ αναλαμπων εκ
του βαθους 'οδηγει παρ'
'ηελιοιο πυλας και δημον
ονειρων

(Transcription by Edward Edinger)

Figure 4. The Bollingen Stone.
(From Aniela Jaffé, *C.G. Jung: Word and Image*)

ferent traditions, because all the traditions have the same source: the unconscious.

In ancient Greece there was a religion called Orphism. The adherents of this religion thought that when they died they would have to make their way a certain distance to reach the gatekeepers. There they would be questioned. If they had the right answers and could say the right things, they would be allowed through the gates into the blessed afterworld. Without the right answers one was not admitted.

So they went to considerable trouble—they carved or engraved on gold tablets (gold, of course, because it wouldn't corrode) the instructions for what the deceased should say to the gatekeepers. Some of those tombs have been discovered; we have rifled their contents, stolen those golden tablets and translated them. Here in part is what they say:

> [After a prelude, when you get to a certain place where some cypress trees are, and you come to the gatekeepers you say this to them:]
>
> I am a child of Earth and of Starry Heaven; but my race is of Heaven.
>
> . . . .
>
> Out of the pure I come, Pure Queen of Them Below,
> Eukles and Eubouleus and the other Gods immortal,
> For I also avow me that I am of your blessed race,
> But Fate laid me low and the other Gods immortal
> . . . . with the starflung thunderbolt.
> I have paid the penalty for deeds unrighteous,
> I have flown out of the sorrowful weary Wheel.
> I have passed with eager feet to the Circle desired.
> I have entered into the bosom of Despoina, Queen of the Underworld.
> Hail, thou who hast suffered the Suffering. This thou hadst never suffered before. Happy and Blessed One, thou shalt be God instead of mortal.
> [And then the final line is the startling one:]
> A kid I have fallen into milk.[33]

You see, one of the basic images in this statement is the image of the divine child. One announces oneself to be a child of earth and starry heaven. So there is a connection with the divine child, the child that comes from heaven. In the final statement the individual announces that he or she has been allowed through the gates; then it is like a child returning to the womb—the kid falling into milk, into boundless nourishment. The deceased confesses to being a child, but not just a child of earth—also a child of heaven. Then one gains admission. So the heavenly knowledge comes out of the mouth of that divine child. It's symbolically analogous to the phrase, "Out of the mouth of babes and sucklings hast thou ordained strength."

Now we have another very important feature in verse 4 of Psalm 8. It's the term "son of man" as distinguished from "man." "What is man, that thou art mindful of him? and the son of man that thou visitest him?" This term "son of man" shows up not only in Psalm 8 but also in Psalm 80:17: "Let thy hand be upon the man of thy right hand, upon the son of man whom thou madest strong for thyself." It shows up in other places, too; in Ezekiel it occurs ninety times! It was also important in the non-canonical Book of Enoch.[34] And in Daniel 7:13-14 we read:

> I saw in the night visions, and, behold, one like the Son of man came with the clouds of heaven, and came to the Ancient of days, and they brought him near before him.
>
> And there was given him dominion, and glory, and a kingdom, that all people, nations, and languages, should serve him: his dominion is an everlasting dominion, which shall not pass away, and his kingdom that which shall not be destroyed.

As you know, this same image, the son of man, is also used many times by Christ. (In the New Testament there are over seventy references to the son of man.) In Matthew 24:30, for instance, he says:

> And then shall appear the sign of the Son of man in heaven: and then shall all the tribes of the earth mourn, and they shall see the Son of man coming in the clouds of heaven with power and great glory.

And again in Matthew 26:24:

> The Son of man goeth as it is written of him: but woe unto that man by whom the Son of man is betrayed! it had been good for that man if he had not been born.

I have a whole book on the history and ramifications of the symbolism of the son of man in the Bible and in ancient Near Eastern sources. It's an image that has occupied Biblical scholars very extensively. One example is an article written in a theological journal some years ago entitled "The Son of Man Again." We're interested in such phenomena psychologically because it indicates that this image has a certain numinosity, an attracting power. Like a magnet, it keeps drawing commentators and thinkers to it—and then, out of the libido that it has activated, they write papers and books.

First of all, the son of man is in more intimate connection with Yahweh than is man since Yahweh *visits* the son of man. Joseph Caryl (1602-1673) interprets visitation as follows:

> *"Thou visitest him."* To visit is, first, to afflict, to chasten, yea, to punish: the highest judgments in Scripture come under the notions of visitations. "Visiting the iniquity of the fathers upon the children" (Ex. xxxiv. 7), that is, punishing them. . . . And it is a common speech with us when a house hath the plague, which is one of the highest strokes of temporal affliction, we use to say, "Such a house is visited." Observe then, afflictions are visitations. . . .
>
> Secondly, to visit, in a good sense, signifies to show mercy, and to refresh, to deliver and to bless; "Naomi heard how that the Lord had visited his people in giving them bread." Ruth i. 6. "The Lord visited Sarah," etc. Gen xxi.1, 2. That greatest mercy and deliverance that ever the children of men had, is thus expressed, "The Lord hath visited and redeemed his people." Luke i. 68. Mercies are visitations; when God comes in kindness and love to do us good, he visiteth us.[35]

I'd like to read you what Augustine says about this term "son of man" as it's used in Psalm 8. Augustine is a remarkable individual psychologically.[36] He was a psychologist without knowing it. Of course he was a theologian, totally contained within the dogmatic framework of the Church—that's unquestionable—and therefore not at all capable of entertaining any heretical viewpoint. He was orthodoxy par excellence. But his quality of relating to the images is far ahead of his time; his associative processes are essentially psychological. Therefore his interpretations often have interesting and valuable psychological points to make. (He goes through all 150 Psalms, verse by verse, commenting on every single one.) Here, somewhat abbreviated, is Augustine's commentary on the 4th verse of Psalm 8:

"What is man, that Thou art mindful of him? or the son of man, that Thou visitest him?" (ver. 4). It may be asked, what distinction there is between man and son of man. . . . This is certainly to be remembered, that every son of man is a man; although every man cannot be taken to be a son of man. Adam, for instance, was a man, but not a son of man. Wherefore we may from hence consider and distinguish what is the difference in this place between man and son of man; namely, that they who bear the image of the earthy man, who is not a son of man, should be signified by the name of men; but that they who bear the image of the heavenly Man, should be rather called sons of men; . . . "Man" then in this place is earthy, but "son of man" heavenly; and the former is far removed from God, but the latter present with God; and therefore is He mindful of the former, as in far distance from Him; but the latter [the son of man] He visiteth [and] enlighteneth him with His countenance. . . .

For [in Psalm 36:6-10] he speaketh thus: "Men and beasts Thou wilt make whole, O Lord, as Thy mercy hath been multiplied, O God. But the sons of men shall put their trust in the covering of Thy wings. They shall be inebriated with the richness of Thine house, and of the torrent of Thy pleasures Thou shalt make them drink. For with Thee is the fountain of life, and in Thy light shall we see light. Extend Thy mercy to them that know Thee." Through the multiplication of mercy then He is mindful of man, as of beasts; for that multiplied mercy reacheth even to them that are afar off; but He visiteth the son of man, over whom, placed under the covering of His wings, He extendeth mercy, and in His light giveth light, and maketh him drink of His pleasures, and inebriateth him with the richness of His house, to forget the sorrows and the wanderings of his former conversation. This son of man, that is, the new man, the repentance of the old man begets with pain and tears.[37]

That's the punch line, worth repeating. "This son of man, that is, the new man, the repentance of the old man begets with pain and tears."

It is rambling, but there's a very interesting point here. There is man, and there is the son of man. God is mindful of man, but he visits the son of man. So he is close to the one he visits, and he just has in mind the other one who is far away from him. The one he visits, he inebriates with the drink and the riches he offers. And then the punch line: "This son of man, that is, the new man, the repentance of the old man begets with pain and tears." You see, man delivers forth a son, the new version of man. And it is out of the pain and tears—out of the pain and tears of Psalm 2 we could say—that the original unregenerate man gives birth to the son of man who is fit to be visited by God. You see how psychological that is, even though it's all couched in religious terminology.

Now this idea of Augustine's that the son of man refers to transformed man has a parallel in Jung's statement concerning God's desire to transform. In "Answer to Job" Jung says: "The father wants to become the son, God wants to become man, the amoral wants to become exclusively good, the unconscious wants to become consciously responsible."[38]

The idea is that when the father-God becomes the son, the appropriate term for that transition will be "Son of God." And we use that term for Christ. But in the Psalm the term is "son of man." Now what is remarkable in the Biblical material is that the Son of God is equated symbolically with the son of man. They are synonymous—and both terms refer to Christ. This has to be psychologically significant. The term "Son of God" symbolizes God's transformation and is equivalent to "Son of man," symbolizing man's—the ego's—transformation. Psychologically I see this to mean that the transformation of the Self is brought about by the transformation of the ego.

Once we get past the terminological differences between "man" and "son of man," then, still in verse 4, we come to the basic question at the core of Psalm 8: what is man? Job, you know, was gripped by that same question. This Psalm doesn't answer it, incidentally. It poses the question but it doesn't answer it. Job also posed it—he was gripped by the question in its practical relation to Yahweh. He asks:

> What is man that you should make so much of him,
>   subjecting him to your scrutiny,
> that morning after morning you should examine him
>   and at every instant test him?

Will you never take your eyes off me
   long enough for me to swallow my spittle?
Suppose I have sinned, what have I done to you,
   you tireless watcher of mankind?
Why do you choose me as your target?
   Why should I be a burden to you? (Job 7:17-20, Jerusalem Bible)

This is the urgent, affect-laden cry: what is man that he must be subjected to the agony of human existence, of *conscious* human existence? And this question is really at the core of the psyche. If you go deeply enough, you will infallibly be stopped dead in your tracks by this. We all spend the greater portion of our lives trying to avoid the question—and if we encounter it, fleeing from it or reaching out for some substitute answer—because it's the ultimate question. It's the riddle of the Sphinx.

Naive Oedipus, you know, thought he'd answered the riddle of the Sphinx. He hadn't at all. The riddle is: "What is it that walks on four legs in the morning, two legs at noon, and three legs in the evening?" And Oedipus very proudly answers, "Ah, the answer is man." He answers one riddle with another! The next question, then, is "All right, what is man?" He didn't go to that next question, so he had to live out his life, you see; that life, and the fruit of that life, is an attempt to answer it.

Alexander Pope (1688-1744) addressed the same question:

Know then thyself, presume not God to scan;
The proper study of Mankind is Man.
Plac'd on this isthmus of a middle state,
A Being darkly wise, and rudely great:
With too much knowledge for the Sceptic side,
With too much weakness for the Stoic's pride,
He hangs between; in doubt to act or rest,
In doubt to deem himself a God, or Beast;
In doubt his Mind or Body to prefer;
Born but to die, and reas'ning but to err;
Alike in ignorance, his reason such,
Whether he thinks too little, or too much:

> Chaos of Thought and Passion, all confus'd;
> Still by himself abus'd, or disabus'd;
> Created half to rise, and half to fall;
> Great lord of all things, yet a prey to all;
> Sole judge of truth, in endless Error hurl'd:
> The glory, jest, and riddle of the world!
>   Go, wondrous creature! mount where Science guides,
> Go, measure earth, weigh air, and state the tides;
> Instruct the planets in what orbs to run,
> Correct old Time, and regulate the sun; . . .
> Go, teach Eternal Wisdom how to rule—
> Then drop into thyself, and be a fool![39]

As I said, Psalm 8—and indeed the entire Bible—does not answer the question, "What is man that thou art mindful of him?" It raises the question, but doesn't answer it. As far as I am concerned, only Jung has answered that question. His answer comes out clearly in "Answer to Job," and I think it is significant that the title contains the word "answer." It comes out perhaps even more succinctly in his wonderful letter to Elinid Kotchnig of June 30, 1956, written in English. In that letter he says:

> Although the divine incarnation is a cosmic and absolute event, it only manifests empirically in those relatively few individuals capable of enough consciousness to make ethical decisions, i.e., to decide for the Good. Therefore God can be called good only inasmuch as He is able to manifest His goodness in individuals. His moral quality depends upon individuals. That is why He incarnates. Individuation and individual existence are indispensable for the transformation of God the Creator.[40]

That's the answer. The answer to the question, "What is man?" Man is the instrument for the transformation of God.

Well now, there's no danger that I've given away a cosmic secret, because that answer will remain just as enigmatic to the vast majority of people who hear it as the question itself—unless and until the individual is ready to discover and experience what that implies for himself. Up to then it's just an empty phrase. But I offer it for those who have ears to hear.

Psalm 14
The Fool Hath Said in His Heart There Is No God

1. The fool hath said in his heart, There is no God. They are corrupt, they have done abominable works, there is none that doeth good.

2. The LORD looked down from heaven upon the children of men, to see if there were any that did understand, and seek God.

3. They are all gone aside, they are all together become filthy: there is none that doeth good, no, not one.

4. Have all the workers of iniquity no knowledge? who eat up my people as they eat bread, and call not upon the LORD.

5. There were they in great fear: for God is in the generation of the righteous.

6. Ye have shamed the counsel of the poor, because the LORD is his refuge.

7. Oh that the salvation of Israel were come out of Zion! when the LORD bringeth back the captivity of his people, Jacob shall rejoice, and Israel shall be glad.

This is a reasonably short Psalm, so let me read the Jerusalem Bible version to give you the flavor of a modern translation:

> The fool says in his heart,
>   'There is no God!'
> Their deeds are corrupt and vile,
>   there is not one good man left.
> Yahweh is looking down from heaven
>   at the sons of men,
> to see if a single one is wise,
>   if a single one is seeking God.
>
> All have turned aside,
>   all alike are tainted;
> there is not one good man left,
>   not a single one.
>
> Are they so ignorant, all these evil men
>   who swallow my people

49

as though they were eating bread,
and never invoke Yahweh?

They will be struck with fear,
fear without reason,
since God takes the side of the virtuous:
deride as you may the poor man's hopes,
Yahweh is his shelter.

Who will bring Israel salvation from Zion?
When Yahweh brings his people home,
what joy for Jacob, what happiness for Israel!

Same Psalm, but somehow in the modern version it's got a different feel.

One of the images that comes out immediately in this Psalm is the image of the fool: "The fool hath said in his heart, there is no God." Now this is an archetypal image and it's part of a pair of opposites: the fool and the wise one. But it sometimes happens, as with all opposites, that a figure wearing the clothing of one is actually doing service for the totality. Just as the wise one often embodies the Self, so too the archetypal image of the fool can sometimes embody wholeness.

In this respect the fool is connected to the image of the divine child. The figure of Parsifal in the Grail Legend is an example. Even though his mother dresses him in "an imaginatively uncouth costume, so that at court he will cut the figure of a gawky, boorish fool," he is described as "a pure fool, through pity wise"[41] and becomes the redeemer of the ailing Grail kingdom. So just because a figure wears the garments of folly or of wisdom doesn't necessarily mean that it stands for only one side of a pair of opposites. Symbolism is fluid in that respect and one must always interpret a given image in terms of the context in which it appears. In the context of Psalm 14, for instance, it is clear that the image of the fool is used as only one side of the pair.

Many Biblical passages are very hard on fools. Here are a few examples: "Let a bear robbed of her whelps meet a man, rather than a fool in his folly." (Prov. 17:12); "As a dog returneth to his vomit, so a fool returneth to his folly." (Prov. 26:11); "Wisdom excelleth folly, as far as light excelleth darkness." (Eccles. 2:13). "A whip for the horse, a bridle for the ass, and a rod for the fool's back." (Prov. 26:3). Proverbs especially does not like fools.

But on the other hand, we have Christ saying: "Whosoever shall say Thou fool, shall be in danger of hell fire." (Matt. 5:22) And there's also Paul's great passage on wisdom and foolishness which is psychologically relevant:

> For the preaching of the cross is to them that perish foolishness; but unto us which are saved it is the power of God.
>
> For it is written, I will destroy the wisdom of the wise, and will bring to nothing the understanding of the prudent.
>
> Where is the wise? where is the scribe? where is the disputer of this world? hath not God made foolish the wisdom of this world?
>
> For after that in the wisdom of God the world by wisdom knew not God, it pleased God by the foolishness of preaching to save them that believe.

Figure 5. A Fool Grimacing.
(Detail of a medieval manuscript; J. Paul Getty Museum, Los Angeles)

> For the Jews require a sign, and the Greeks seek after wisdom:
> But we preach Christ crucified, unto the Jews a stumbling block, and
> unto the Greeks foolishness;
> But unto them which are called, both Jews and Greeks, Christ the
> power of God, and the wisdom of God.
> Because the foolishness of God is wiser than men; and the weakness of
> God is stronger than men. . . .
> But God hath chosen the foolish things of the world to confound the
> wise; and God hath chosen the weak things of the world to confound the
> things which are mighty;
> And base things of the world, and things which are despised, hath God
> chosen, yea, and things which are not, to bring to nought things that are.
> (1 Cor. 1:18-28)

Man's wisdom is God's foolishness, and man's foolishness is God's wisdom. In this passage it's a matter of enantiodromia: one side of a pair of opposites can reverse and turn into its contrary. You see, the ego, insofar as it sets itself up against the Self, is submitting to foolishness. And yet, for the modern mind, it is a necessary foolishness because it corresponds to the necessary crime upon which ego development is based. We will come back to this later.

There is another very interesting feature to this Psalm. Verse 5 reads: "There were they in great fear: for God is in the generation of the righteous." The Jerusalem translation reads: "They will be struck with fear, fear without reason, since God takes the side of the virtuous." The Douay Version—the English translation of the Vulgate— reads: "They have not called upon the Lord; there have they trembled for fear, where there was no fear." This passage is important psychologically, and it's reminiscent of a passage in Deuteronomy 28. Here, Moses is speaking to the disobedient children of Israel:

> For not obeying the voice of Yahweh your God, just as Yahweh took de-
> light in giving you prosperity and increase, so now he will take delight in
> bringing you ruin and destruction. You will be torn from the land which
> you are entering to make your own. Yahweh will scatter you among all
> peoples, from one end of the earth to the other; there you will serve other
> gods of wood and of stone that neither you nor your fathers have known.

Among these nations there will be no repose for you, no rest for the sole of your foot; Yahweh will give you a quaking heart, weary eyes, halting breath. Your life from the outset will be a burden to you; night and day you will go in fear, uncertain of your life. In the morning you will say, "How I wish it were evening!", and in the evening, "How I wish it were morning!", such terror will grip your heart, such sights your eyes will see. (Deut. 28:63-67, Jerusalem Bible)

And again, in Leviticus:

And if, in spite of this, you do not listen to me but set yourselves against me, I will set myself against you in fury and punish you sevenfold for your sins. . . . (Lev. 26:27-28, Jerusalem Bible)

I will strike fear into the hearts of those of you that are left; in the land of their enemies the sound of a falling leaf shall send them fleeing as men flee from the sword, and they shall fall though there is no one pursuing them. (Lev. 26:36, Jerusalem Bible)

Just as "they will be struck with fear, fear without reason."

These passages all belong to the psychology of phobias—fears without apparent reason, anxiety attacks, flight when no one is pursuing you. If we look for the archetypal basis of phobic symptoms we will generally find the picture that's described in these passages from Deuteronomy and Leviticus. "Yahweh will give you a quaking heart, weary eyes, halting breath." In other words, the victim of phobia has been given a quaking heart not by an external danger but by the inner complex whose archetypal core is the Self.

Now that's not how it first looks when one starts to analyze such a case. At first it usually looks as if the phobia comes from some traumatic childhood experience. Perhaps the person was terrorized by a violent father as a child. If one is satisfied with that personalistic level of interpretation, then that's as far as the issue will go—the childhood experience will continue to repeat itself in adult life and one will circle endlessly around it. But the problem is never really settled on the personal childhood level. It gets settled only when the dreams lead to the underlying archetypal level of what's expressed here in the statement that Yahweh is giving the person a quaking heart. It may be true that originally the father gave the child a quaking heart. But that's not the root of the matter.

At the core, the childhood experience is just a particular example of the universal, archetypal experience of man's relation to Yahweh, the ego's relation to the Self. The child happened to encounter that wrathful aspect prematurely, precociously. It's too much for a child to have to encounter so much so soon. But reality isn't nice about such things—too often it happens whether or not the person is ready for it. The root of the problem is not the father; the root of the problem is Yahweh or, psychologically, the Self. As I have written elsewhere, "Behind a . . . parent problem will lurk the dynamism of the Self. . . . All problems of alienation . . . are ultimately alienation between ego and Self."[42] And these Biblical references illustrate and amplify that fact.

Finally, Psalm 14 is used as a proof-text for the doctrine of original sin. It says explicitly in verses 2 and 3 that there's not a single person on earth who isn't sinful:

> The LORD looked down from heaven upon the children of men, to see if there were any that did understand, and seek God. They are all gone aside, they are all together become filthy: there is none that doeth good, no, not one.

Well, that's about as total as one can get, and therefore I'd say that's a pretty good text for original sin. Paul quotes this passage in Romans 3:12, and Paul is the fountainhead of the Christian doctrine of original sin.[43] There are also other references in the Psalms that say the same thing. For example in Psalm 143:2 we read that "in thy sight shall no man living be justified."

Understood psychologically, these are not matters for theoretical or doctrinal dispute. The psychological approach transcends all those matters because it penetrates to the psychic facts underlying all doctrines. In this particular case the psychological fact is that individual existence, based on the development of an individual ego-consciousness, is a crime. According to whom? According to what? Well, it is a crime according to the nature of the psyche. The unconscious describes it as a crime. And the religious and mythological materials simply illustrate how the unconscious psyche speaks of the emergence of the ego.

Ego-consciousness presumes to exist as an autonomous center of being. Consciousness could not come into being if the individual ego did not make that assumption. In order to exist at all, it is obliged to set itself up against the unconscious from which it has been born. It takes the energies of the instincts belonging to the natural psyche—the energies of desire, of pleasure, of power—and appropriates them to itself. And those energies then go to build up ego existence as a separate center of being. What's more, all civilized societies must support the assumption that the ego is autonomous. And so, as individuals, we are treated as though we are each completely responsible for all our actions. Ridiculous of course—we're doing things all the time without any notion of where they come from, or why. But society is constructed to support individual consciousness and thereby it promotes the original crime.

The ego's claim to be an autonomous center of being—that, symbolically, is the rebellion of Lucifer, "the son of the morning"![44] It is the dawn of the ego. It is the original sin and applies to everybody. Because it occurs contrary to the original natural state of things, ego existence is by nature guilt-laden. It is not possible to live a guilt-free life and have any degree of consciousness—they go together. All that is implicit in the imagery of this Psalm.

Psalm 22
The Suffering Servant

This is a particularly important Psalm. It's rather long, so I will focus on the first 21 verses.

1. My God, my God, why hast thou forsaken me? why art thou so far from helping me, and from the words of my roaring?

2. O my God, I cry in the daytime, but thou hearest not; and in the night season, and am not silent.

3. But thou art holy, O thou that inhabitest the praises of Israel.

4. Our fathers trusted in thee: they trusted, and thou didst deliver them.

5. They cried unto thee, and were delivered: they trusted in thee, and were not confounded.

6. But I am a worm, and no man; a reproach of men, and despised of the people.

7. All they that see me laugh me to scorn: they shoot out the lip, they shake the head, saying,

8. He trusted on the LORD that he would deliver him: let him deliver him, seeing he delighted in him.

9. But thou art he that took me out of the womb: thou didst make me hope when I was upon my mother's breasts.

10. I was cast upon thee from the womb: thou art my God from my mother's belly.

11. Be not far from me; for trouble is near; for there is none to help.

12. Many bulls have compassed me: strong bulls of Bashan have beset me round.

13. They gaped upon me with their mouths, as a ravening and a roaring lion.

14. I am poured out like water, and all my bones are out of joint: my heart is like wax; it is melted in the midst of my bowels.

15. My strength is dried up like a potsherd; and my tongue cleaveth to my jaws; and thou hast brought me into the dust of death.

16. For dogs have compassed me: the assembly of the wicked have inclosed me: they pierced my hands and my feet.

17. I may tell all my bones: they look and stare upon me.

18. They part my garments among them, and cast lots upon my vesture.

19. But be not thou far from me, O LORD: O my strength, haste thee to help me.

20. Deliver my soul from the sword; my darling from the power of the dog.

21. Save me from the lion's mouth: for thou hast heard me from the horns of the unicorns.

This is the crucial turning point, the exclamation of release: "Thou hast heard me from the horns of the unicorns." I've been heard! I was hanging on the horns of the unicorn—in other words, I was in desperate circumstances—and you heard me. The rest of the Psalm is praise and thanksgiving for having been heard and released.

Figure 6. Unicorn miniature from *Physiologus,* ca. 12th century.
(From Rüdiger Robert Beer, *Unicorn: Myth and Reality)*

This Psalm, along with Psalms 2 and 110, is one of the major Messianic Psalms. As we saw in Psalm 2, the Old Testament's anticipation of the coming of the Messiah had in it the basic idea that the Messiah would come twice. Sometimes, in the legendary material, it is expressed a little differently—there will be two Messiahs. Either way, symbolically the coming of the Messiah is a double event: the second coming will be in glory and victory as in Psalm 2; but the first coming, described in Psalm 22, is in humiliation and defeat.

Christ, you know, quoted the beginning of this Psalm on the cross: "My God, my God, why hast thou forsaken me?" Some think that he quoted the entire Psalm. That's a kind of fantasy—all the patristic symbolisms are amplificatory fantasies—and they tell us something. The idea that Christ may have quoted the entire Psalm on the cross tells us that the Crucifixion amplifies, lives out, Psalm 22. In fact, that is evident in the Gospel story, because in it there are so many images—such as casting for lots—which are taken from Psalm 22.

This Psalm has many similarities of theme and substance to a passage in Isaiah called the Suffering Servant passage. I want to read that to you because it is so important psychologically. Here is the Jerusalem Bible version:

See, my servant will prosper,
he shall be lifted up, exalted, rise to great heights.

As the crowds were appalled on seeing him
—so disfigured did he look
that he seemed no longer human—. . . .

a thing despised and rejected by men,
a man of sorrows and familiar with suffering,
a man to make people screen their faces;
he was despised and we took no account of him.

And yet ours were the sufferings he bore,
ours the sorrows he carried.
But we, we thought of him as someone punished,
struck by God, and brought low.
Yet he was pierced through for our faults,
crushed for our sins.

On him lies a punishment that brings us peace,
and through his wounds we are healed. (Isa. 52:13-14; 53:3-5)[45]

Well, of course this is also a Messianic passage, and it is precisely the same image we find in Psalm 22:6 where the Messiah says of himself: "I am a worm and no man; a reproach of men, and despised of the people."

Here is an absolutely astonishing juxtaposition of two images. This is the Messiah speaking; the coming king of the universe; the culmination, salvation and justification of the whole human race. The most superlative value and meaning was attributed to the Messiah. And the Messiah is describing himself as a worm! It staggers the imagination, yet here it is.

Now this image appears in other places, too—psychological facts are never isolated phenomena. That is, in fact, how we discover archetypal reality: similar images are found in many different places and in different guises. So I'll pursue this further because it needs to be understood psychologically.

The image of the worm leads us to the Egyptian myth of the phoenix. Here is what *Physiologus,* an early medieval book of legends and folklore (written around 200 A.D.), says about the phoenix:

> There is a species of bird in the land of India which is called the phoenix, which enters the wood of Lebanon after five hundred years and bathes his two wings in the fragrance. He then signals to the priest of Heliopolis . . . during the new month. . . . When the priest has been signaled, he goes in to the altar and heats it with brushwood. Then the bird enters Heliopolis laden with fragrance and mounts the altar, where he ignites the fire and burns himself up. The next day then the priest examines the altar and finds a worm in the ashes. On the second day, however, he finds a tiny birdling. On the third day he finds a huge eagle which taking flight, greets the priest and goes off to his former abode.

Physiologus then goes on to give us a moral:

> If this species of bird has the power to kill himself in such a manner as to raise himself up, how foolish are those men who grow angry at the words of the Savior, "I have the power to lay down my life and I have the power

to take it again" [John 10:18]. The phoenix represents the person of the Savior since, descending from the heavens, he left his two wings full of good odors (that is, his best words) so that we, holding forth the labors of our hand might return the pleasant spiritual odor to him in good works. Physiologus, therefore, speaks well of the phoenix.[46]

So the phoenix is equated with the Messiah and with Christ. (Indeed, in medieval iconography, the phoenix is a symbol for the Resurrection of Christ.)[47] And one stage of the life cycle of the phoenix is the worm stage.

This is complicated. But, to avoid arbitrary statements, one must make the effort to present the psychological data on which the statements rest. This of course accounts for the difficulty of Jung's later works. He is demonstrating to us the empirical method of studying the archetypal psyche. Difficult though it is, there is no other way to lay out the empirical facts so as to separate them from arbitrary opinion—and there is no field as subject to confusion between opinion and fact as the field of psychology.

Coming, as it does, from Egypt, the phoenix myth clearly relates to Egyptian embalming symbolism. That symbolism has to do with death and rebirth—the whole Egyptian civilization was obsessed with death and with death's transformative consequences. In fact, the basic purpose of the embalming process was to create an immortal body—Osiris. That is also the basic root of alchemy. Psychologically, the transformation of the phoenix symbolizes the transformation process of individuation which creates, as the alchemists would say, a "glorified indestructible body," the eternal fruit or product of a consciously lived life.

One of the symbolic meanings of the worm image is death. When we die we become food for the worms. We don't see that in modern times because we don't have dead corpses lying around the way they did in the Middle Ages. But it used to be a vivid experience for people—death turned the body into a mass of wriggling worms. This is one of the phases of the life cycle of the phoenix; and, as Psalm 22 says, it's one of the phases of the life cycle of the Messiah.[48]

Now, since the alchemists were concerned with the same basic psychological facts, the same imagery comes up in the description of what happens to the *prima materia.* For instance, here's an example from an alchemical text:

> Again, as our chemical compound . . . is subjected to the action of fire, and is decomposed, dissolved, and well digested, and as this process, before its consummation, exhibits various chromatic changes, so this Divine Man, and Human God, Jesus Christ, had, by the will of His heavenly Father, to pass through the furnace of affliction, that is, through many troubles, insults, and sufferings, in the course of which His outward aspect was grievously changed. . . .
>
> Then again, the Sages have called our compound, while undergoing the process of decomposition, the Raven's Head, on account of its blackness. In the same way, Christ [i.e., the Suffering Servant of Isaiah] had no form nor comeliness—was despised and rejected of men—a man of sorrows and acquainted with grief—so despised, that men hid, as it were, their faces from Him.[49]

This is an alchemical recipe that describes the transformation of the *prima materia* in the alchemical retort—often in the form of the king who must be reborn. The *materia* is subject to the same death and rebirth sequence endured by the phoenix and by the Messiah. It must undergo a state of tortured *mortificatio.*[50] This takes us to the astonishing idea that the reborn king in alchemy, the reborn Yahweh in Christ or in the Messiah, and the reborn phoenix—all those entities are variations of the same psychic fact. All appear first as a worm.

I want to give you another example of the same imagery. It comes from an unpublished letter of Jung's, quoted by Gerhard Adler. In it Jung says this:

> The problem of crucifixion is the beginning of individuation; there is the secret meaning of the Christian symbolism, a path of blood and suffering—like any other step forward on the road of the evolution of human consciousness. Can man stand a further increase of consciousness? . . . I confess that I submitted to the divine power of this apparently unsurmountable problem and I consciously and intentionally made my life miserable, because I wanted God to be alive and free from the suffering man

has put on him by loving his own reason more than God's secret intentions.[51]

I bring this in because it is another example of the transformative aspect of misery, the creative aspect of being a worm.

This takes us to the phenomenology of the opposites—the way they work. But *only* if there is enough consciousness to know what is going on. (Notice that Jung says "consciously and intentionally"). Otherwise it doesn't work. This can all go terribly astray, so be careful how you take what I say here. Don't take it too literally or concretely.

In the long run, nature requires a balance. In the short run there can be terrible imbalances, but not in the long run. If one is gripped by an extreme state of one side of a pair of opposites, that experience is something like being pushed down onto a compressed spring. Extreme one-sidedness propels you with equal force in the opposite direction. That's what happens in the worm-Messiah equation. To feel utterly humiliated presses you down onto the coiled spring of the opposites and then you will be thrown over to the opposite—supreme glory.

That is the way it works if one is possessed by archetypal energy and the ego doesn't know what is happening. If there is no consciousness, the ego can be tossed helplessly back and forth on that coiled spring. This dynamism is the making of psychoses, you know. But, to the extent that you have some conscious insight into how this dynamism operates, you can more willingly accept whatever experiences you encounter. If you have something approaching a worm experience, and you are aware that it is part of a larger pattern, you can bear it. Contrariwise, if you encounter an experience where you are glorified too much, you will be very apprehensive because you know that that, too, is a coiled spring which will throw you back to the worm. Consciousness of the larger pattern mitigates the experience considerably; it keeps the spring from coiling too tightly and throwing you too far. But still, it's difficult work.

The Messiah-worm duality is the union of the highest and lowest. One can understand that as an idea—it is not hard to say the words and to grasp the idea abstractly—but it is exceedingly difficult to handle experientially. When one is in the midst of the worm experience, even if one is conscious, there is an overwhelming tendency to identify with it. One is utterly worthless, despicable and of no significance—just something that can be crushed underfoot. What is smaller and baser than a worm? One really feels that way about oneself, when that image is experientially activated. Yet, in order to have the authentic experience, you must, to some degree, identify with it. Otherwise, you can say, "Oh well, this is just that union of opposites archetype here; I don't have to take this seriously." That's *sublimatio*[52]—being above it all. Then nothing happens. There is no fire, no suffering, no transformation, no reborn phoenix, no coming of the Messiah. One must feel the heat.

Again, the only ultimate safety in these matters is consciousness: knowing what one is dealing with—the shape of the larger pattern and the dynamism of the opposites. Then, one hopes, a recognition of the nature of what grips you will not deprive you of the experience but will bring with it sufficient orientation to prevent a complete inundation. Dreams are usually of immense help in this regard. When one is consciously identified with the worm state, one is very likely to have a compensatory dream which points to the other side of the equation. Or the reverse: when one is inflated, identified with an overvaluation, a worm dream may come. And that also is very salutary. You may not like it, but it's good for you.

Jung has a fine passage in *Mysterium Coniunctionis* that can help one from taking it too personally. He is discussing how the alchemists equated the Philosophers' Stone with Christ, and how the various ordeals the *materia* had to go through were equated with Christ's Passion. Then he says:

If the adept experiences his own Self, the "true man," in his work, then ... he encounters the analogy of the true man—Christ—in new and direct form, and he recognizes in the transformation in which he himself is involved a similarity to the Passion. It is not an "imitation of Christ" but its exact opposite: an assimilation of the Christ-image to his own Self, which is the "true man."[53] It is no longer an effort, an intentional strain-

ing after imitation, but rather an involuntary experience of the reality represented by the sacred legend. . . . The Passion *happens* to the adept, not in
its classic form . . . but in the form expressed by the alchemical myth. It
is the arcane substance that suffers those physical and moral tortures; it is
the king who dies or is killed, is dead and buried and on the third day
rises again. And it is not the adept who suffers all this, [that's what keeps
the objective attitude so the ego doesn't identify with it. It doesn't have
be tossed back and forth on that coiled spring] rather *it* [the *materia*] suffers in him, *it* is tortured, *it* passes through death [it's the worm so to
speak] and [*it*] rises again. All this happens not to the alchemist himself
but to the "true man," who he feels is near him and in him and at the
same time in the retort.[54]

In other words, it's the transformation of the Self, the Anthropos,[55]
that is taking place within the individual.

Figure 7. Christ as Anthropos, flanked by the four elements.
(From Glanville, *Pe Propriétaire des choses,* 1482)

Psalm 23
The Good Shepherd

We now turn to the best known Psalm in the Psalter, Psalm 23. We couldn't leave that one out. And it is appropriate that it follow Psalm 22 because it compensates a broken state of being.

1. The LORD is my shepherd; I shall not want.

2. He maketh me to lie down in green pastures: he leadeth me beside the still waters.

3. He restoreth my soul: he leadeth me in the paths of righteousness for his name's sake.

4. Yea, though I walk through the valley of the shadow of death, I will fear no evil: for thou art with me; thy rod and thy staff they comfort me.

5. Thou preparest a table before me in the presence of mine enemies: thou anointest my head with oil; my cup runneth over.

6. Surely goodness and mercy shall follow me all the days of my life: and I will dwell in the house of the LORD for ever.

Recently, there have been quite a number of new translations of the Bible. (This in itself is an interesting psychological phenomenon.) I've followed these with interest and have read the reviews as each one has been published. To the best of my recollection, whenever a new translation of the Old Testament comes out, just about every reviewer uses for comparison the standard King James Version of the twenty-third Psalm. That gives you a sense of how important this Psalm is collectively.

I want to read you an eloquent encomium for Psalm 23 written by the well-known nineteenth-century preacher, Henry Ward Beecher (1813-1887). You can understand from this why he packed them in with his sermons! Listen to this:

David has left no sweeter Psalm than the short twenty-third. It is but a moment's opening of his soul; but, as when one, walking the winter

65

street, sees the door opened for some one to enter, and the red light streams a moment forth, and the forms of gay children are running to greet the comer, and genial music sounds, though the door shuts and leaves the night black, yet it cannot shut back again all that the eyes, the ear, the heart, and the imagination have seen—so in this Psalm, though it is but a moment's opening of the soul, are emitted truths of peace and consolation that will never be absent from the world. The twenty-third Psalm is the nightingale of the Psalms. It is small, of a homely feather, singing shyly out of obscurity; but, oh! it has filled the air of the whole world with melodious joy, greater than the heart can conceive.

Blessed be the day on which that Psalm was born! What would you say of a pilgrim commissioned of God to travel up and down the earth singing a strange melody, which, when one heard, caused him to forget whatever sorrow he had? And so the singing angel goes on his way through all lands, singing in the language of every nation, driving away trouble by the pulses of the air which his tongue moves with divine power.

Behold just such an one! This pilgrim God has sent to speak in every language on the globe. It has charmed more griefs to rest than all the philosophy of the world. It has remanded to their dungeon more felon thoughts, more black doubts, more thieving sorrows, than there are sands on the sea-shore. It has comforted the noble host of the poor. It has sung courage to the army of the disappointed. It has poured balm and consolation into the heart of the sick, of captives in dungeons, of widows in their pinching griefs, of orphans in their loneliness. Dying soldiers have died easier as it was read to them; ghastly hospitals have been illuminated; it has visited the prisoner, and broken his chains, and, like Peter's angel, led him forth in imagination, and sung him back to his home again. It has made the dying Christian slave freer than his master, and consoled those whom, dying, he left behind mourning, not so much that he was gone, as because they were left behind, and could not go too.

Nor is its work done. It will go singing to your children and my children, and to their children, through all the generations of time; nor will it fold its wings till the last pilgrim is safe, and time ended; and then it shall fly back to the bosom of God, whence it issued, and sound on, mingled with all those sounds of celestial joy which make heaven musical for ever.[56]

You see, the basic image of this Psalm is the image of the Good Shepherd. And what Henry Ward Beecher is referring to, I think, is the fact that this Psalm constellates that archetypal image and conveys its effect. In other words, it speaks to the unconscious of the individual in need and activates the shepherding, nourishing aspect of the Self. It is a feature of that phenomenology that it will work most powerfully when the need for what it offers is greatest. If everything is fine, you'll just stay on the surface of it and say, "Isn't that nice." Nice words, nice sentiments—but if one isn't open, they don't strike to the archetypal depths. Only when the need is great do they really hit home.

This image of the Good Shepherd belongs to antiquity. It is found not only in the Old Testament; it is also found in the symbolism of Orpheus, and in some of the symbolism of Hermes, too. We have ancient images of the Good Shepherd carrying a lamb on his shoulder—that's the most common image. Perhaps the lamb is hurt; that isn't stated but it is likely. Hermes was associated with the Good Shepherd in his role as psychopomp, as guide or shepherd of souls. A similar figure also shows up in the hermetic writings attributed to Hermes Trismegistus (Thrice Greatest Hermes): a figure called *poimandres,* the shepherd of men (Figure 8, next page). And then, of course, the major symbolic development of the Good Shepherd took place in the symbolism of Christ.

The classic text that identifies Christ with the Good Shepherd is found in the Gospel of John. I want to read that to you. This is Christ speaking:

I tell you most solemnly, anyone who does not enter the sheepfold through the gate, but gets in some other way is a thief and a brigand. The one who enters through the gate is the shepherd of the flock; the gatekeeper lets him in, the sheep hear his voice, one by one he calls his own sheep and leads them out. When he has brought out his flock, he goes ahead of them, and the sheep follow because they know his voice. They never follow a stranger but run away from him: they do not recognise the voice of strangers.

. . . .

Figure 8. The Poimandres, Shepherd of Men.
(Museum of the Acropolis, Athens)

I tell you most solemnly,
I am the gate of the sheepfold.
All others who have come
are thieves and brigands;
but the sheep took no notice of them.
I am the gate.
Anyone who enters through me will be safe:
he will go freely in and out
and be sure of finding pasture.
The thief comes
only to steal and kill and destroy.
I have come
so that they may have life
and have it to the full.
I am the good shepherd:
the good shepherd is one who lays down his life for his sheep.
The hired man, since he is not the shepherd
and the sheep do not belong to him,
abandons the sheep and runs away
as soon as he sees a wolf coming,
and then the wolf attacks and scatters the sheep;
this is because he is only a hired man
and has no concern for the sheep.
I am the good shepherd;
I know my own
and my own know me,
just as the Father knows me
and I know the Father;
and I lay down my life for my sheep. (John 10:1-15, Jerusalem Bible)

This theme of the sheep and the shepherd comes up in dreams every now and then. A particularly good example is one told by Jung. I shall read it because it also gives me a chance to quote some of Jung's commentary from a seminar—it has a flavor of Jung different from his formal writings. In this seminar, Jung discusses a series of visions of a patient in her early thirties. The process began with several key dreams, and this is one of them:

I was in a boat with some man. He said, "We must go to the very end of the lake, where the four valleys converge, where they bring down the flocks of sheep to the water." When we got there, he found a lame sheep in the flock, and I found a little lamb that was pregnant. It surprised me because it seemed too young to be pregnant. We tenderly took those two sheep in our arms and carried them to the boat. I kept wrapping them up. The man said, "They may die, they are shivering so." So I wrapped them up once more.[57]

Even though I've gone through these seminars carefully, an idea just came to me as I was reading this dream, an idea that hadn't been quite conscious before. You see, this dream shows the patient, together with the good shepherd, jointly caring for the sheep. I think now, since this was practically an initial dream for these seminars, that it's a picture of all the work she herself did on the visions, before those seminars. That work was her caring for the sheep.

Here we have the image—doubled, actually—of the good shepherd carrying the sheep, the same image that we find in antiquity with the sheep on his shoulders. So knowing that, it is immediately evident that this is an archetypal dream, also because of the extraordinary feature of the four valleys converging at one spot—a mandala image. As part of my amplification of Psalm 23, I want to read you some of Jung's comments about this dream.

The man assumes the role of the good shepherd. . . . He guides the dreamer to the place of the four valleys and when he comes to his flock picks up a lame sheep. He is a figure that can be likened to a very interesting figure of the primitive church, called the *Poimen,* which has now vanished from ecclesiastical terminology. The good shepherd has remained, but the other figure has vanished with a certain book that was almost canonical at the time called *The Shepherd of Hermas.*[58] When the New Testament writings were gathered together, that was omitted. I must use the Greek word *Poimen* here because this *Poimen* is a pre-Christian figure. . . . It is a pagan invention, and has a direct historical relation to Orpheus . . . another figure related to Christ. Orpheus . . . was understood to be an anticipation of Christ because he tamed wild passions in the form of wild animals by his delicate music. He is also like a shepherd, and moreover he is called "the Fisher," and as such he played a great role in the Dionysian mysteries. . . . So we see the Christ figure in heathen cults. We even find in certain inscriptions Christ almost identical with Bacchus, absolutely on the same level.[59]

I would draw your attention here to the allusive way in which Jung presents himself in his seminars. He allows himself great amplitude in elaborating the various interconnections of an archetypal image. Here he starts out talking about the good shepherd and then he wanders away, because he's weaving a network of interconnected images. But he knows exactly where he is—he never gets lost. And then when he's finished one piece, he goes back to the center where he started from and proceeds out again:

Caligula, that famous perverted Emperor, had a sanctuary where he kept the images of the great Gods, and Christ was one of them; for of course in the early days the figure of Christ was quite hazy, our idea of him is an absolutely new invention.

In very early times he was not a person at all, and so he was always handled in that way—symbolized accordingly. So for instance, the form of the *Poimen* was a sort of tremendous big angel, of more than human size, a great invisible spirit, a good God, and that very impersonal figure was never called Christ. That name was taboo. He was called the Shepherd of Men—Poimandres, the great leader of men, a mystery man, but directly related to *The Shepherd of Hermas,* which is decidedly Christian and part of the early Christian literature until the fifth or sixth century. We have the pagan form in a very interesting Greek text, and the best idea I can give you of that is that it is a book which might have been written by an analytical patient about his visions. . . . It was a man who wrote it because the mysteries were then chiefly a man's business. Today they are a woman's business.[60]

Let me stop here a minute because that is very true: "Today they are a woman's business." What Jung means is that at present it is the women who are capable of going deepest in analysis. That's uniformly true in my work. Men can't go to the same depth as women can—they are too afraid of the psyche. Jung just slips that in, you see, on the basis of his experience. He continues:

Now our good lady has of course not the least idea of what she is dreaming. It is just that unknown man who picks up the sheep, but you see as a matter of fact she returns here to the archetypal pattern really of the spirit-like leader of men. It goes right back to the spirit-leaders of primitive tribes—where certain men called medicine men are at times possessed by spirits, chiefly ancestral spirits, who lead them and tell what is good for the people.[61]

Look what Jung does here: this is the impressive thing about Jung's seminars. He touches all bases, covers all areas. He's been talking about the classical Greek reference to the *poimen*, then about the Orphic reference, then the Christian reference and finally the Shepherd of Hermas. And now he shifts to primitive psychology, another area where archetypal images are still in living view. The conscious ego has not so eclipsed them as to make them invisible. Jung goes on:

There is a marvelous example in that book by Rasmussen about his experiences among the Polar Eskimos in the north of Greenland.[62] He gives there a striking case where part of those Polar Eskimos, foreseeing starvation, were led by a medicine man who had had a vision, across by Baffin's Bay to the North American continent where they reached food. Now that man had never been there and nobody knew that they could get across the sea, yet he succeeded in convincing the tribe. He had a vision that the Happy Land was there. In the winter when Baffin's Bay was frozen over, they started to travel across. Half way over, part of the tribe began to doubt, they said there was nothing ahead and decided to return, and they died of starvation. The other half he led safely across. This describes exactly what the shepherd or medicine man means under primitive circumstances. It is an intuitive mind possessed by a vision, clairvoyance.[63]

All of that applies to Psalm 23. When one is in desperate circumstances psychologically, the primitive aspect of the psyche is open and activated—one is very much like those starving Eskimos. If one then follows one's instinct, it will lead to whatever manifestation of the Good Shepherd comes along. And often, as Henry Ward Beecher describes so well, that manifestation is Psalm 23.

The Psalm speaks of still waters: "He leadeth me beside the still waters." Augustine interprets these as the waters of baptism.[64] The still waters are saving waters. We would say psychologically that the Good Shepherd aspect of the Self leads the open and responsive ego to the water of life. But if for an individual that image, that vital energy, happens to be contained within the symbolism of a particular religious framework, then it will be that body of religious imagery which will have the enlivening effect. That's the way it was for Augustine. Thus, he interprets the still waters that the Good Shepherd leads one to as the waters of baptism leading into the Church, because it was absolutely right for his psychology. It won't be right for the majority of modern psychologically-oriented people—we have to think it through in more psychological terms—but it was right for him, and symbolically it's the same thing. You see, whatever symbolic image works and has the living effect, no matter where one locates it, "restoreth my soul." You find it where it is for you.

"The valley of the shadow of death," Augustine equates with this life.[65] That's another typical orthodox Christian tendency: projecting into the afterlife the fruit of the transformation. You endure the death part in the hell of this life and then the good part comes in the afterlife, so this life is called the shadow of death.

As I have said, the Good Shepherd aspect of the Self leads the open and responsive ego to the water of life. The necessary descent into the unconscious is part of the encounter with that water—it's a night sea journey. Although it is experienced in part as going through the valley of the shadow of death, one learns by that experience that the helpful aspect of the Self is encountered there. Jung is fond of quoting some lines of Hölderlin because they express such a fundamental psychic truth: "Wherever danger is, there grows also the rescuing power." So it is in the valley of the shadow of death that you encounter the Good Shepherd aspect of the Self.

This Psalm speaks first of the Good Shepherd aspect and then takes you to the valley of the shadow of death. Usually it's experienced the other way around: you stumble into the valley of the shadow without knowing how you got there, but while there you encounter the Good Shepherd. That is the experience that forges a living, confidence-generating connection between the ego and the guidance of the Self.

Finally, Psalm 23 is an example of the banquet archetype: "Thou preparest a table before me in the presence of mine enemies." The Last Supper is also an image of the banquet archetype,[66] as is the eucharistic ritual of the Church, which celebrates the Last Supper. The Jewish legend of the Messianic Banquet at which Leviathan and Behemoth will be served up is another example.[67] Additional examples are the totem meal of primitives, the Passover meal, the manna and quail eaten in the wilderness, and Plato's dialogue entitled *The Banquet* (also known as the *Symposium,* but I think "banquet" is a better translation.)

All these images refer basically to the same psychological fact, namely to the nourishing and celebratory aspect of the Self. Why do I say celebratory? Because the very term "banquet" indicates it's no ordinary meal. A banquet is a special meal, and a meal that is arranged under the circumstances described in Psalm 23 is no everyday meal if it is served by God himself, by the Good Shepherd! It is nourishing, but that term doesn't do justice to the nature of what's being described. This is a celebratory occasion that makes the partaker a participant in the divine process because, you see, its divine food that's being offered. That's true in the symbolism of the Mass and it's also true in the symbolism of the Messianic Banquet.

This image comes up not uncommonly in dreams. Sometimes the food that's served at that banquet is very disagreeable—and that's one aspect of the celebrative quality too. It can be unusual in its disagreeable nature as well as being nectar and ambrosia.

Psalm 51
The Miserere

"A Psalm of David, when Nathan the prophet came unto him,
after he had gone in to Bathsheba."

1. Have mercy upon me, O God, according to thy loving kindness: according unto the multitude of thy tender mercies blot out my transgressions.

2. Wash me thoroughly from mine iniquity, and cleanse me from my sin.

3. For I acknowledge my transgressions: and my sin is ever before me.

4. Against thee, thee only, have I sinned, and done this evil in thy sight: that thou mightest be justified when thou speakest, and be clear when thou judgest.

5. Behold, I was shapen in iniquity; and in sin did my mother conceive me.

6. Behold, thou desirest truth in the inward parts: and in the hidden part thou shalt make me to know wisdom.

7. Purge me with hyssop, and I shall be clean: wash me, and I shall be whiter than snow.

8. Make me to hear joy and gladness; that the bones which thou hast broken may rejoice.

9. Hide thy face from my sins, and blot out all mine iniquities.

10. Create in me a clean heart, O God; and renew a right spirit within me.

11. Cast me not away from thy presence; and take not thy holy spirit from me.

12. Restore unto me the joy of thy salvation; and uphold me with thy free spirit.

13. Then will I teach transgressors thy ways; and sinners shall be converted unto thee.

14. Deliver me from bloodguiltiness, O God, thou God of my salvation: and my tongue shall sing aloud of thy righteousness.

15. O Lord, open thou my lips; and my mouth shall shew forth thy praise.

16. For thou desirest not sacrifice; else would I give it: thou delightest not in burnt offering.

17. The sacrifices of God are a broken spirit: a broken and a contrite heart, O God, thou wilt not despise.

18. Do good in thy good pleasure unto Zion: build thou the walls of Jerusalem.

19. Then shalt thou be pleased with the sacrifices of righteousness, with burnt offering and whole burnt offering: then shall they offer bullocks upon thine altar.

The Miserere is perhaps the major one of a number of so-called penitential Psalms. It is a prayer of contrite repentence, confession of sins, and a request for forgiveness. So this Psalm brings up the whole question of confession and penitence: the place it has played in the Church, and also the part it plays psychologically. Confession is a major dynamic in the process of psychotherapy.

Jung gives us some essential information on this subject in a talk he gave in 1939 called "The Symbolic Life." He was speaking informally in English to the Guild of Pastoral Psychology in London—to people interested in religious matters. Referring to religious dogma, he says this:

> The sad truth is that we do not understand it any more. But, you know, in former centuries man did not need that kind of intellectual understanding. We are very proud of it; but it is nothing to be proud of. Our intellect is absolutely incapable of understanding these things. We are not far enough advanced psychologically to understand the truth, the extraordinary truth, of ritual and dogma. Therefore such dogmas should never be submitted to any kind of criticism. [As long, of course, as the dogmas are still alive for us.]
>
> So, you see, if I treat a real Christian, a real Catholic, I always keep him down to the dogma, and say "You stick to it! And if you begin to criticize it in any way intellectually, then I am going to analyse you, and then you are in the frying-pan!" When a practising Catholic comes to me, I say, "Did you confess this to your father-confessor?" Naturally he says, "No, he does not understand." "What in hell, then," I say, "did you confess?" "Oh, lousy little things of no importance"—but the main sins

he never talked of. As I said, I have had quite a number of these Catholics—six. I was quite proud to have so many, and I said to them, "Now, you see, what you tell me here, this is really serious. You go now to your father-confessor and you confess, whether he understands or does not understand. That is of no concern. It must be told before God, and if you don't do it, you are out of the Church, and then analysis begins, and then things will get hot, so you are much better off in the lap of the Church." So, you see, I brought these people back into the Church, with the result that the Pope himself gave me a private blessing for having taught certain important Catholics the right way of confessing.

For instance, there was a lady who played a very great role in the war. She was very Catholic, and always in the summer she used to come to Switzerland to pass her summer holiday. There is a famous monastery there with many monks, and she used to go to it for confession and spiritual advice. Now, being an interesting person, she got a bit too interested in her father-confessor, and he got a bit too interested in her, and there was some conflict. He was then removed to the Clausura (the part of the religious house from which those of the opposite sex are excluded), and she naturally collapsed, and she was advised to go to me. So she came to me in full resistance against the authorities who had interfered, and I made her go back to her spiritual authorities and confess the whole situation. And when she went back to Rome, where she lived, and where she had a confessor, he asked her, "Well, I know you from many years ago: how is it that you now confess so freely?" And she said she had learnt it from a doctor. That's the story of how I got the Pope's private blessing.

My attitude to these matters is that, as long as a patient is really a member of a church, he ought to be serious. He ought to be really and sincerely a member of that church, and he should not go to a doctor to get his conflicts settled when he believes that he should do it with God. For instance, when a member of the Oxford Group comes to me in order to get treatment, I say, "You are in the Oxford Group; so long as you are there, you settle your affair with the Oxford Group. I can't do it better than Jesus."[68]

As Jung puts it, you see, only if one is *not* contained in a particular dogmatic creed is analysis to be considered. And it will only be under such circumstances that you'll be able to follow me further in some of the things I have to say about this Psalm—because I say some rather radical things so far as the traditional viewpoint is concerned.

Before we get into that, just a few words about Jung's teaching Catholics how to confess. The confession is the prelude to partaking of the mystery of the Eucharist. In order for that experience to be authentic, psychologically alive, it must be genuine. That means the content of the confession must be something one is *really* ashamed of, *genuinely* guilty about. That is very easy to discover, because it will be whatever one least wants to tell. Just think to yourself, "What would I least want to get up on my feet right now and tell to this assembled group." Something will spring to mind, I promise you! And the same applies also in analysis: what you most fear to let your analyst in on is precisely what you should bring to the analytic hour. Then the analysis is alive. (Incidentally, I don't recommend collective confession. I just use that fantasy as an example to help individuals locate what it is they're not comfortable about in themselves.)

Anyway, for a practicing Catholic, whatever one doesn't feel comfortable about, especially in relation to God and the Church, is what one must bring to the confessional. Then it will be alive and there will be a chance for authentic absolution, a real experience of being saved from a state of guilt. And as long as that works, as Jung says, it shouldn't be touched.

What I am going to turn to now can only be followed if one does not look at this material from a religious point of view but is open to considering what it implies psychologically. Something very startling is implied by this Psalm.

Psalm 51 is about that matter of sin, guilt, confession. And as the initial statement at the beginning tells us, it has to do with David's sin in relation to Bathsheba and Uriah—a very ugly episode. I'll remind you of the essence of it.

David, from the rooftop of his palace, spied beautiful Bathsheba and fell into an infatuation with her. She was inconveniently—for him—married to Uriah, one of his army officers. To gratify his lust for Bathsheba, David had her husband Uriah murdered by having him assigned to a particularly dangerous area in the battlefield and then abandoned. David then took Bathsheba as one of his wives. (2 Sam. 11) That's a story concerning one of the most illustrious figures of the Old Testament—David.

Let me slip in here one psychological meaning that is immediately apparent from this story. It may seem a little too abstract, but I'm going to slip it in as part of the interpretation. In terms of this story as a psychological drama, if David is the ego, then Bathsheba—the anima—is married to the shadow—Uriah—who's in a subordinate position of being a soldier. The ego wants the gratification of union with the anima but goes about that desire illegitimately, because one cannot relate to the anima or animus by attempting to bypass the shadow. This is a basic psychological theme—it's almost routine in the garden variety of positive anima or animus projections—but it is not legitimate. What we call falling in love is a positive anima or animus projection. In the grips of it, one is possessed by a kind of blissful, paradisiacal illusion of an ideal state of harmony. But that illusion is bought at the price of murdering—repressing—the shadow. Sooner or later it makes its way back up, the illusion is shattered, and consequences unfold. That is one way of interpreting the David and Bathsheba story.

Now let's look at it from other angles. A Jewish legend tells the following story:

> One day as David sat in his chamber, writing a psalm, Satan came into the room disguised as a bird. Its feathers were of pure gold, its beak of diamonds, and its legs of glowing rubies. David dropped his book and tried to catch the bird which he thought had come from the Garden of Eden. But the bird flew out of the window and settled upon the low branch of a tree in a neighboring garden. And under the branch of the tree a young woman was washing her hair. [She was Bathsheba and David took her by arranging the death of her husband Uriah.][69]

David's interest then shifted from the bird to Bathsheba, and things proceeded. You see this bird (Satan in disguise), coming as it does from the Garden of Eden, corresponds with what I said about the paradisiacal, illusory nature of the anima or animus projection.

According to another legend, it was God, not David, who brought about his crime with Bathsheba, in order that God might then say to other sinners "Go to David and learn how to repent."[70]

These two legends give us another way of looking at the whole story. I have linked them together because, psychologically understood, Satan and God are two aspects of the same numinous phenomenon. And according to the first story, the bird was encrusted with precious jewels—which indicates that major psychological values were embodied by the figure of the bird, Satan. That's always what jewels symbolize in dreams. So you begin to see how ambiguous the story becomes. It loses its simple black and white quality.

Furthermore, we learn from the legend that the bird came from the Garden of Eden. In other words, the bird is a messenger from that state of original wholeness. On the one hand this symbolizes a regressive longing for the blissful origin from which—according to that myth—we have all been exiled. On the other hand, however, it points to the potential connection with wholeness, consciously achieved, which is equivalent to the reconstitution of the Garden of Eden—Paradise.

The second legend says that God, not David, was behind it all, and that God did it so he could say to other sinners, "Go to David and learn how to repent."[71] This gives us a key to accepting our own sins and mistakes, a very difficult thing to do. It's much easier to accept somebody else's sins against oneself; it's very difficult to accept one's own sins or mistakes.

You notice I use two different terms. What's the difference between a sin and a mistake? It's a sin from the feeling point of view; it's a mistake from the thinking point of view. Often people express their guilty deeds as "mistakes." That's why Plato can say—I guess Buddha said the same thing—that all sin comes down to ignorance. Just a mistake—one didn't happen to know—so the whole feeling dimension is put aside; there's no such thing as guilt. That's the thinking person's conclusion, you see.

As a thinker, I have every bit as much trouble accepting a mistake as I do a sin, because they are essentially of the same nature psychologically. What they do, in effect, is humiliate the ego. They are an experience of defeat for the ego. If the ego is striving to be good and right and correct, according to whatever its precepts are, a sin is a failure. And if the ego has consciousness—knowing what it's doing—as a major value, then if it makes a mistake of any proportion, that is likewise a humiliating failure.

As I said earlier, this legend gives us the key that may help us accept such things. It says that God brought about David's crime in order to use him as an example of how to repent. Not an example of how to commit a crime, but an example of how to repent, an example of how the transformation process works. A mistake or a crime acknowledged, suffered and lived through, can have a transformative effect on the individual who did it. It can be accepted insofar as it has provided an impetus for one's own psychological development and transformation. It's not an example for anybody else, but an internal example. It really does work that way. And when you begin to see it in that light, you begin to see sins and mistakes as a necessary part of psychological development.

The Biblical material itself also implies that David's crime was necessary, because the fruit of his union with Bathsheba is the ancestor of the Messiah. Solomon was the fruit of that union, and the Christian genealogies for Christ take him back to Solomon and to David and Jesse. In Jewish legends likewise, the future Messiah (not identified with Christ—it's a different symbolic context) also comes via the line of David and Solomon. So, according to those symbolic genealogies, the crime was necessary.

A twelfth- or thirteenth-century manuscript illumination shows Nathan confronting David for his sin, and David's repentence (Figure *V*, next page) I think of David's story as a particularly good example of the psychic life cycle (Figure 10, page 83).

The fact is that one cannot have repentence, one cannot enter the transformative developmental cycle, without sin—a rather hard and dangerous doctrine, but true. According to certain Gnostic sects, one cannot be redeemed from a sin one does not commit. *Very* dangerous doctrine. And it had better not be taken literally. Yet it expresses the

Figure 9. The Penitence of David.
(Illumination from a Byzantine manuscript)

truth that one must pay real attention to the shadow, give it profound acceptance—with all the sinfulness, with all the guilt it generates—if the individuation process is to proceed. Otherwise, if one remains just safely settled in the good, the right—whatever one has determined "right" to be—then psychological growth stops.

Now I'm not through with this, because more radical psychological conclusions can be drawn from this Psalm. In verse 4, David speaks to Yahweh: "Against thee, thee only, have I sinned, and done this evil in thy sight: that thou mightest be justified when thou speakest, and be clear when thou judgest."

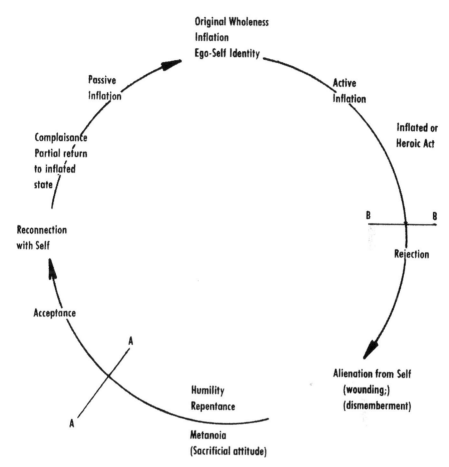

Figure 10. The Psychic Life Cycle.

Augustine's Bible says almost the same thing: ". . .that thou mayest be justified in thy saying and conquer when thou art judged." This passage was a problem to Augustine, and it's an example of his honest effort to face the data that show up in the Scriptures. I want to read you part of his comment to show you what he does with it. He slips out of it by virtue of his religious container:

"Against Thee alone have I sinned and before Thee an evil thing have I done." What is this? For before men was not another wife debauched and husband slain? Did not all men know what David had done? What is, "Against Thee alone have I sinned and before Thee an evil thing have I done?" Because Thou alone art without sin. He is a just punisher that hath nothing in Him to be punished; He is a just reprover that hath nothing in Him to be reproved. "That Thou mayest be justified in Thy sayings, and conquer when thou art judged." To whom he speaketh brethren, to whom he speaketh, is difficult to understand. [Right!] To God surely he speaketh, and it is evident that God the Father is not judged.[72]

Well, that's not evident at all; he is making an assumption as to the nature of God. That's the difficulty when individuals are contained in a particular creedal framework. They think they know the nature of God. They think they've got him defined, caught in their formula; therefore if there's a God-image that doesn't fit the formula, then they can say, "Oh, that's not God, because God the Father is not judged."

Here's how Augustine gets out of it: he solves the problem by concluding that it refers not to God the Father, but to Christ:

> What is, "And conquer when Thou art judged"? He seeth the future Judge [i.e., Christ] to be judged, one just by sinners to be judged, and therein conquering, because in Him was nothing to be judged. . . .To Him then, having no sin, saith on the present occasion the Prophet David, "Against Thee only have I sinned, and before Thee an evil thing have I done, that Thou mayest be justified in Thy sayings, and conquer when Thou art judged." For Thou overcomest all men, all judges; and he that deemeth himself just, before Thee is unjust: Thou alone justly judgest, having been unjustly judged, That hast power to lay down Thy life, and hast power again to take it. Thou conquerest, then, when Thou art judged. All men Thou overcomest, because Thou art more than men, and by Thee were men made.[73]

He goes on and it's very interesting. I don't have time to go into it, but I wanted at least to show you how he tries to engage the issue. At that time, the particular God-image was what it had to be; it could not be otherwise. Therefore we are not entitled to criticize what it was for that time. But now we can see—with the help of psychology—that in this passage of the Psalm, the astonishing realization is dawning (even though it took another two thousand years for it to come into full view) that God is justified by man. It says that. "Against Thee only have I sinned and done this evil in thy sight that Thou mayest be justified when Thou speakest and be clear when Thou judgest." In other words, contrary to what Augustine said, God *is* judged. I don't think anybody can read "Answer to Job" without admitting that Jung judged Yahweh. I don't think you can escape that. A dangerous operation, I admit, but he did it.

You see, psychologically, the time has now come—just barely—when we can entertain the idea of a process in which the ego takes responsibility for the evil promptings of the Self, in order that the Self may be transformed.

Taking all this material together—the text itself, the legendary material and Augustine's comments—psychologically we can say that the motivation for a crime of this nature, a crime of passion, derives from Yahweh. One of the legends even says that. But it is ambiguous and difficult for religious commentators, because it requires one to understand that Yahweh is two-sided, a union of opposites. What happens psychologically is that David commits his crime out of a temporary possession by the unconscious, and then takes conscious responsibility for his behavior in order that God may be justified. In other words the ego takes conscious responsibility—accepting guilt and repentence—for the evil promptings of the primordial Self, so that the Self may be transformed.[74] And the embryo of that idea is in the Psalm 51.

A similar idea is expressed in *The Rubaiyat of Omar Khayyam*, written in the eleventh century. Edward Fitzgerald translated it from Persian into English in the nineteenth century. I'm not sure whether or not this is an absolutely accurate translation, but I assume Fitzgerald didn't make it up and must have gotten it out of *The Rubaiyat*.[75] Let me read it to you:

> Oh Thou, who didst with pitfall and with gin
> Beset the Road I was to wander in,
>   Thou wilt not with Predestined Evil round
> Enmesh, and then impute my Fall to Sin!

Oh Thou, who Man of baser Earth didst make,
And e'en with Paradise devise the Snake:
For all the Sin wherewith the Face of Man
Is blacken'd—Man's forgiveness give—and take![76]

Question: Could you say more about the "transformation of God"?

Edinger: I'm not sure what to say briefly that will be meaningful. Of course, it is a very startling idea to speak of the transformation of God. Shocking! What can that possibly mean? It is easier if one speaks in more modest terms about the transformation of the unconscious, as one works on the encounter with it.[77] The process of the encounter between the conscious ego and those affective realities of the unconscious does bring about transformations.

The whole symbolism of alchemy has to do with that one word: transformation. Alchemy is a transformation mystery. And although it is not explicit, the data is clear in the alchemical material that the *prima materia* they started with was identified with God.[78] So just on the basis of alchemical data alone—the symbolic data—one has reason to speak of the transformation of God.

Now the hard part is to make the bridge to one's personal life experience—to apply those ideas and symbolic images. I don't think I can do that successfully for individuals in a collective lecture setting. It's just not possible. It takes years of analysis just to approach it. But there's no harm in putting out these ways of thinking. They're provocative; and they may drop into the unconscious of certain individuals and perhaps germinate. In the future, some experience or a dream may bring this matter up again, and you'll say "Oh that's what he meant!" But don't expect utter clarity, because there is no such thing—not in this field anyway.

So, if you don't understand it, that's all right. I don't understand it either. But I have reached a formulation that more or less satisfies me for the moment. The hard part, of course, comes when one has to live out what one is talking about with these words. That's the hard part.

Psalm 63
The Thirsty Soul

"A Psalm of David when he was in the wilderness of Judah."

1. O God, thou art my God; early will I seek thee: my soul thirsteth for thee, my flesh longeth for thee in a dry and thirsty land, where no water is;

2. To see thy power and thy glory, so as I have seen thee in the sanctuary.

3. Because thy loving kindness is better than life, my lips shall praise thee.

4. Thus will I bless thee while I live: I will lift up my hands in thy name.

5. My soul shall be satisfied as with marrow and fatness; and my mouth shall praise thee with joyful lips:

6. When I remember thee upon my bed, and meditate on thee in the night watches.

7. Because thou has been my help, therefore in the shadow of thy wings will I rejoice.

8. My soul followeth hard after thee: thy right hand upholdeth me.

9. But those that seek my soul, to destroy it, shall go into the lower parts of the earth.

10. They shall fall by the sword: they shall be a portion for foxes.

11. But the king shall rejoice in God; every one that sweareth by him shall glory: but the mouth of them that speak lies shall be stopped.

This Psalm is supposed to have been composed when David was in the wilderness. There would be two possible occasions for that in the history of David: his period in the wilderness when he was being persecuted by Saul—before he became king; or alternatively, his later period of exile during the rebellion of his son Absalom. The commentators seem to agree that the use of the term "king" in verse 11 refers to King David. So if he is already king, it would indicate that the Psalm comes from his second wilderness experience. In either case, it refers psychologically to the state of ego-Self alienation which usually precedes an experience of the Self.

If we consider that Psalm 63 comes from David's wilderness experience during Absalom's rebellion, we are led back to Psalm 51. In 2 Samuel 12:11, Yahweh says to David that in punishment for his crime against Uriah, "Behold, I will raise up evil against thee out of thine own house." And that evil was the rebellion of Absalom. It's a complicated story that involved incest and reprisal for incest. The net result was that Absalom rebelled against David and tried to take over the government. As a consequence, David was temporarily ousted from his kingship and fled to the wilderness.

As I mentioned in my remarks about Psalm 51, David's story was in my mind when I charted what I call the Psychic Life Cycle. David is an outstanding example of that whole sequence because, as king, he succumbed to hubris and committed the crime. But then he went through the whole cycle; he didn't just perish because of the crime. By being able to repent, he carried it through and, following a wilderness experience, he was reinstated again. So I see Psalm 63 as directly connected to Psalm 51. That's one reason I selected them both.

One commentator says this about Psalm 63:

Hagar saw God in the wilderness, and called a well by the name derived from that vision, *Beer-lahai-roi.* Gen. xvi. 13, 14. Moses saw God in the wilderness. Exod. iii. 1-4. Elijah saw God in the wilderness. 1 Kings xix. 4-18. David saw God in the wilderness. The Christian church will see God in the wilderness. Rev. xii. 6-14. [The reference to Rev. 12 speaks of a woman clothed with the sun bringing forth a man child and then fleeing into the wilderness to escape a dragon (Figure 11).] Every devout soul which has loved to see God in his house will be refreshed by visions of God in the wilderness of solitude, sorrow, sickness, and death.[79]

That's an eighteenth-century remark illustrating what I refer to psychologically as the encounter with the Self in a state of ego-Self alienation.[80] And this is what the Psalm refers to. You see, thirst for contact with the numinous becomes acute during the experience of the wilderness.

Augustine says that the wilderness or desert mentioned in the Psalm refers to "this world":

Figure 11. The Woman of the Apocalypse.
(Illumination from *The Cloisters Apocalypse,* ca. 1310-1320;
Metropolitan Museum of Art, New York)

This life, wherein we suffer so great toils, and wherein to so great necessities we are made subject . . . even here is a desert where there is much thirst, and ye are to hear the voice of One now thirsting in the desert. But if we acknowledge ourselves as thirsting, we shall acknowledge ourselves as drinking also. For he that thirsteth in this world, in the world to come shall be satisfied, according to the Lord's saying, "Blessed are they that hunger and thirst after righteousness, for the same shall be satisfied." (Matt. 5:6) Therefore in this world we ought not to love fulness. Here we must thirst, in another place we shall be filled. But now in order that we may not faint in this desert, He sprinkleth upon us the dew of His word, and leaveth us not utterly to dry up.[81]

This is a classical expression of the traditional Christian standpoint that belittles this world and glorifies the world to come. But here Augustine is speaking of the opposites: emptiness and fullness, thirsting and satisfaction. The fullness is projected into the afterlife, while the thirst is applied to this concrete earthly existence.

Now, in terms of psychological understanding, this is the basic flaw of traditional Christianity. The opposites are split, you see. This life—the existence of the ego, life on earth, material coagulated being—is associated with emptiness and evil. The ultimate good is projected into the afterlife. But this impoverishes earthly existence!

I think it is indisputable that this division was essential for the development of the collective psyche. In order for the spiritual standpoint to develop, to stand over against just raw material being, it had to undervalue all that was earthly and physical. But nevertheless, that can't pass muster by modern psychological standards. Therefore, it is the *union* of opposites—which includes and values concrete ego existence—that is affirmed by depth psychology.

This idea or image of being thirsty in a desert is the same image used by a modern-day psalmist. I refer to T.S. Eliot. Let me read you a few lines from "The Waste Land" that strike exactly the same note:

> What are the roots that clutch, what branches grow
> Out of this stony rubbish? Son of man,
> You cannot say, or guess, for you know only
> A heap of broken images, where the sun beats,

And the dead tree gives no shelter, the cricket no relief,
And the dry stone no sound of water.
. . . .
Here is no water but only rock
Rock and no water and the sandy road
The road winding above among the mountains
Which are mountains of rock without water
If there were water we should stop and drink
Amongst the rock one cannot stop or think
Sweat is dry and feet are in the sand
If there were only water amongst the rock
Dead mountain mouth of carious teeth that cannot spit
Here one can neither stand nor lie nor sit
There is not even silence in the mountains
But dry sterile thunder without rain
There is not even solitude in the mountains
But red sullen faces sneer and snarl
From doors of mudcracked houses[82]

Authentic poets, you know, give expression to the *Zeitgeist,* the spirit of the times. In my opinion, "The Waste Land" is a picture of the current state of the collective psyche.

This thirst of the soul in Psalm 63 brings to mind a fine passage by Emerson. In "The Over-Soul," he says this:

The argument which is always forthcoming to silence those who conceive extraordinary hopes of man, namely the appeal to experience, is forever invalid and vain. We give up the past to the objector, and yet we hope. He must explain this hope. We grant that human life is mean, but how did we find out that it was mean? What is the ground of this uneasiness of ours; of this old discontent? What is the universal sense of want and ignorance [the sense of thirst], but the fine innuendo by which the soul makes its enormous claim?[83]

You see, if we experience a thirst, a want, a need—if that experience comes out of our biology, our built-in, innate patterns of reaction—then it implies that something must exist to satisfy that want. That's Emerson's idea. Our sense of want is the "fine innuendo by which the soul makes its enormous claim." And David thirsts for Yahweh: "My soul thirsteth for thee."

In a more general sense, the symbol of thirst brings up the whole matter of desirousness, and the psychological importance of that cannot be overestimated. In alchemy it is symbolized by sulphur.[84]

There is a wonderful section in *Mysterium Coniunctionis* which begins in a way identical to Psalm 63. This is a unique passage, in that Jung takes an alchemical text and then proceeds to interpret it in detail, psychologically. There's no other place, to my knowledge, where he does that. If you want to have an idea of what a personal analysis with Jung would have been like, read this particular passage.[85] He speaks directly to the reader as though he or she had this alchemical text as a dream, and it's quite a marvelous passage. I'm going to read you a little bit of it because it refers directly to the symbolism of Psalm 63. The alchemical text he interprets begins like this:

> If thou knowest how to moisten
> this dry earth with its own water,
> thou wilt loosen the pores of the earth.

So the text starts out with a state of dryness, a state of thirst that needs to be moistened. It goes on, but let me read some of what Jung says about it because it belongs to the whole symbolism of thirst— frustrated desirousness, longing and deprivation—thirst at different levels of being. Jung says:

> If you will contemplate your lack of fantasy, of inspiration and inner aliveness, which you feel as sheer stagnation and a barren wilderness, and impregnate it with the interest born of alarm at your inner death, then something can take shape in you, for your inner emptiness conceals just as great a fulness if only you will allow it to penetrate into you. [In other words, the "fulness" isn't projected into the afterlife.] If you prove receptive to this "call of the wild,"[86] the longing for fulfilment will quicken the sterile wilderness of your soul as rain quickens the dry earth. (Thus the Soul to the Laborant, staring glumly at his stove and scratching himself behind the ear because he has no more ideas.) . . . .
> You are so sterile because, without your knowledge, something like an

evil spirit has stopped up the source of your fantasy, the fountain of your soul. The enemy is your own crude sulphur, which burns you with the hellish fire of desirousness, or *concupiscentia.* You would like to make gold because "poverty is the greatest plague, wealth the highest good." You wish to have results that flatter your pride, you expect something useful, but there can be no question of that as you have realized with a shock. Because of this you no longer even *want* to be fruitful, as it would only be for God's sake but unfortunately not for your own. . . .

Therefore away with your crude and vulgar desirousness, which childishly and shortsightedly sees only goals within its own narrow horizon. Admittedly sulphur is a vital spirit . . . an evil spirit of passion; . . . useful as it is at times, it is an obstacle between you and your goal. The water of your interest is not pure, it is poisoned by the leprosy of desirousness which is the common ill. You too are infected with this collective sickness. Therefore bethink you for once, "extrahe cogitationem" [literally, "stretch what you know"] and consider: What is behind all this desirousness? A thirsting for the eternal, which as you see can never be satisfied with the best. . . . The more you cling to that which all the world desires, the more you are Everyman, who has not yet discovered himself and stumbles through the world like a blind man leading the blind with somnambulistic certainty into the void where all the paralyzed ones follow him.[87] Everyman is always a multitude. Cleanse your interest of that collective sulphur which clings to all like a leprosy. For desire only burns in order to burn itself out, and in and from this fire arises the true living spirit which generates life according to its own laws, and is not blinded by the shortsightedness of our intentions or the crude presumption of our superstitious belief in the will.[88]

I'll repeat the core message here: "What is behind all this desirousness?" Answer: "A thirsting for the eternal." And, you see, that's the point David has arrived at in the wilderness. He has been deprived of all that would bring him concrete earthly satisfaction. His son has turned against him, he's lost his kingdom and he's an exile in the wilderness. And so all he has left is a thirst for the eternal, namely for Yahweh.

Psalms 69 and 130
The Call from the Depths

As Psalm 69 and Psalm 130 concern the same theme, I'm going to take them together. Psalm 69 is a long Psalm, and the part I want to talk about is the first nine verses. But Psalm 130 is short so I'll read it in its entirety.

Psalm 69: *Salvum Me* (Save Me)

1. Save me O God; for the waters are come in unto my soul.

2. I sink in deep mire, where there is no standing: I am come into deep waters, where the floods overflow me.

3. I am weary of my crying: my throat is dried: mine eyes fail while I wait for my God.

4. They that hate me without a cause are more than the hairs of mine head: they that would destroy me, being mine enemies wrongfully, are mighty: then I restored that which I took not away.

5. O God, thou knoweth my foolishness; and my sins are not hid from thee.

6. Let not them that wait on thee, O Lord GOD of hosts, be ashamed for my sake: let not those that seek thee be confounded for my sake, O God of Israel.

7. Because for thy sake I have borne reproach; shame hath covered my face.

8. I am become a stranger unto my brethren, and an alien unto my mother's children.

9. For the zeal of thine house hath eaten me up; and the reproaches of them that reproached thee are fallen upon me.

Psalm 130: *De Profundis* (Out of the Depths)

1. Out of the depths have I cried unto thee, O LORD.

2. Lord, hear my voice: let thine ears be attentive to the voice of my supplications.

3. If thou, LORD, shouldest mark iniquities, O Lord, who shall stand?

4. But there is forgiveness with thee, that thou mayest be feared.

5. I wait for the LORD, my soul doth wait, and in his word do I hope.

6. My soul waiteth for the Lord more than they that watch for the morning: I say, more than they that watch for the morning.

7. Let Israel hope in the LORD: for with the LORD there is mercy, and with him is plenteous redemption.

8. And he shall redeem Israel from all his iniquities.

These two Psalms are particularly important psychologically because they picture so vividly the dangerous state of the ego being overwhelmed by the unconscious. Let us consider just such a situation and reflect on it a bit.

When the ego is swamped by the unconscious, it is an urgent crisis. And as the Psalms demonstrate, in such a situation it's psychologically real and correct—indeed quite necessary—to reach out for whatever can bring a sense of order; to reach out for centering, calming and consolidation. Very often the images that emerge to fulfill this function are images of wholeness, and that's how I understand what the psalmist is calling out for. He's calling out to Yahweh to rescue him from the depths, from sinking into the mire. Yahweh, as an expression of the God-image, is an image of the Self, the totality—wholeness. And in psychological experience this usually appears explicitly as a mandala image.

Jung gives us such a concise and lucid description of what I'm talking about that I'm going to read it to you. Analytical psychology has a lot of fancy words, a lot of Latinisms that can intimidate the unscholarly. The matters it deals with, however, are elemental, simple, basic. And under many circumstances those basic matters are the crucial ones. I don't care that you already know this material, because you know it and you don't know it. You know it until the next time you fall into a hole in the unconscious—then you don't know it at all. And maybe you'll be reminded at such a time where this passage is to be found. Here's what Jung says:

The Sanskrit word *mandala* means "circle" in the ordinary sense of the word. In the sphere of religious practices and in psychology it denotes circular images, which are drawn, painted, modelled, or danced. Plastic structures of this kind are to be found, for instance, in Tibetan Buddhism, and as dance figures these circular patterns occur also in Dervish monasteries. As psychological phenomena they appear spontaneously in dreams, in certain states of conflict, and in cases of schizophrenia. Very frequently they contain a quaternity or a multiple of four, in the form of a cross, a star, a square, an octagon, etc. In alchemy we encounter this motif in the form of the *quadratura circuli* [squaring of the circle].

In Tibetan Buddhism the figure has the significance of a ritual instrument (*yantra*), whose purpose is to assist meditation and concentration. Its meaning in alchemy is somewhat similar, inasmuch as it represents the synthesis of the four elements which are forever tending to fall apart. Its spontaneous occurrence in modern individuals enables psychological research to make a closer investigation into its functional meaning. As a rule a mandala occurs in conditions of psychic dissociation or disorientation ["I am come into deep waters, where the floods overflow me"], for instance in the case of children between the ages of eight and eleven whose parents are about to be divorced, or in adults who, as the result of a neurosis and its treatment, are confronted with the problem of opposites in human nature and are consequently disoriented; or again in schizophrenics whose view of the world has become confused, owing to the invasion of incomprehensible contents from the unconscious. In such cases it is easy to see how the severe pattern imposed by a circular image of this kind compensates the disorder and confusion of the psychic state—namely, through the construction of a central point to which everything is related, or by a concentric arrangement of the disordered multiplicity and of contradictory and irreconcilable elements. This is evidently an *attempt at self-healing* on the part of Nature, which does not spring from conscious reflection . . . .

The "squaring of the circle" is one of the many archetypal motifs which form the basic patterns of our dreams and fantasies. But it is distinguished by the fact that it is one of the most important of them from the functional point of view. Indeed, it could even be called the *archetype of wholeness*. Because of this significance, the "quaternity of the One" is the schema for all images of God, as depicted in the visions of Ezekiel, Daniel, and Enoch, and as the representation of Horus with his four sons also shows.[89]

Well, this is what happens in Psalm 69. David is calling out for a connection with the central point to which everything is related—an image of God that will provide him with the healing effects generated by a mandala. In *The Visconti Hours* there is a lovely illumination at the beginning of Psalm 69 (Figure 12). The first letter of the Psalm is an S—*Salvum me*, "Save me" is how it begins. In the lower portion of the S, King David is about to drown in the sea; and in the upper part

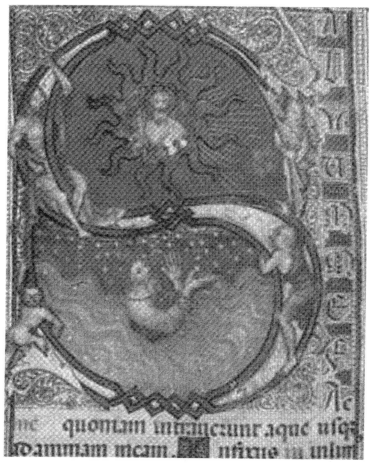

Figure 12. The Illuminated Letter S at the Beginning of Psalm 69. (From *The Visconti Hours;* National Library, Florence)

of the S, Yahweh is in a circle with the rays of the sun coming out of it. Yahweh looks down on David and David looks up at Yahweh, calling to him. David is calling out for rescue; the integrity of the ego is threatened. He's asking for a mandala symbol of wholeness to come to him so that the ego won't be inundated by the unconscious.

Once again, I want to bring in an alchemical reference. Maybe this is a good time to mention why I think the alchemical references are so important. What we're trying to do is translate into psychological, experiential terms the images that have been embedded in a metaphysical, dogmatic, religious framework.

What makes alchemy so valuable for depth psychology is that it is a prelude to the psychological viewpoint. It is a pre-psychological viewpoint which took these same images from classical mythology, and from the Old and New Testaments, and reapplied them to what was going on in the alchemical retort. So the alchemists have already done part of our work; they've used their crowbars to extract these images and move them into another setting—an alchemical setting. With that work done, it is possible for the psychological standpoint to take it one step further. It would be much harder if we didn't have that intermediary alchemical step. That's why alchemy is so valuable for depth psychology, why it meant so much to Jung, and why I keep referring to it.

As is so often the case, we have an alchemical text that makes use of the same imagery as appears in Psalms 69 and 130. It even quotes both Psalms. In *Mysterium Coniunctionis* Jung comments on a passage from the alchemical text, *Aurora Consurgens*. In the text, the Shulamite of the Song of Songs is speaking; she is a personification of the *prima materia* that is being worked on in the alchemical vessel:

> Be turned to me with all your heart and do not cast me aside because I am black and swarthy, because the sun hath changed my colour and the waters have covered my face and the land hath been polluted and defiled in my works; for there was darkness over it, because I stick fast in the mire of the deep [a direct quote from Psalm 69] and my substance is not disclosed. Wherefore out of the depths have I cried [a direct quote from Psalm 130: *De profundis clamavi ad te*—"Out of the depths have I cried to thee"], and

from the abyss of the earth with my voice to all you that pass by the way. Attend and see me, if any shall find one like unto me, I will give into his hand the morning star.[90]

These are the very words of Psalms 69 and 130, taken out of the mouth of the psalmist and put into the mouth of the personification of the *prima materia*—the unconscious—who is calling out to be rescued from the mire of the deep in which she's stuck! Look what the alchemists were up to; look what they've done. Their unconscious, and the whole creative process that caught them up, has taken this particular Biblical material and transposed it into a new format. So now it is not David who needs rescuing, nor the human being—psychologically, the ego—but the Shulamite, the unconscious. And the rescuer now is not Yahweh; the rescuer is to be the alchemist. The *prima materia* is calling out to the alchemist: "Do your laboratory work so you can rescue me."

You see, the transposition has taken place and the responsibility now rests with the human ego. So it's not just a matter of the ego being rescued by the Self—that of course is one theme and there are plenty of occasions when that is called for. But in alchemy a whole different set-up occurs in which the *ego* takes on the task of rescuing the *prima materia* in the darkness. And, as we saw in Psalm 51, certain texts in alchemy explicitly equate the *prima materia* with God,[91] so the whole process becomes reversed: in the Psalms, David calls out to God to rescue him from the depths; in the alchemical context, God is lost in the darkness and calls out to the alchemist for rescue.

That shows how complex and paradoxical these images are—and how easy it can be, then, for an individual to become lost or disoriented. It is paradoxical and indeed ridiculous, if not blasphemous, to think of God mired in the depths and in need of rescue. But it wasn't my idea. That's what makes it safe—it is not my personal idea! It is there in the material and I just point it out, that's all.

Now let me read what Jung has to say about this:

The "mire of the deep" refers to Psalm . . . [69:2]: . . . "I sink in deep mire, where there is no standing." David's words are interpreted by

Epiphanius [an early Church Father] as follows: there is a material which consists of "miry reflections" and "muddy thoughts of sin." But of Psalm 130:1: "Out of the depths have I cried to thee, O Lord," he gives the following interpretation: "After the saints are so graced that the Holy Ghost dwells within them, he gives them, after having made his habitation in the saints, the gift to look into the deep things of God, that they may praise him from the depths, as also David declares: 'Out of the depths,' he says, 'have I cried to thee, O Lord.' "[92]

You see, there are two interpretations: one is "Help me, I'm sinking into the deep mire," and the other is that the saints are graced by the experience of the depths, in order that they can praise God out of the depths—a very different way of looking at it. Jung goes on to say:

These contradictory interpretations of the "depths" *(profunda)* come very much closer together in alchemy, often so close that they seem to be nothing more than two different aspects of the same thing. It is natural that in alchemy the depths should mean now one and now the other, to the despair of all lovers of consistency. But the eternal images are far from consistent in meaning. It is characteristic of the alchemists that they never lost sight of this polarity, thereby compensating the world of dogma, which, in order to avoid ambiguity, emphasizes the one pole to the exclusion of the other. The tendency to separate the opposites as much as possible and to strive for singleness of meaning is absolutely necessary for clarity of consciousness, since discrimination is of its essence. But when the separation is carried so far that the complementary opposite is lost sight of, and the blackness of the whiteness, the evil of the good, the depth of the heights, and so on, is no longer seen, the result is one-sidedness, which is then compensated from the unconscious without our help.[93]

Out of all of this comes the idea that the experience of the depths referred to in Psalms 69 and 130 is not single, but double. It is not just the experience of desperate fear of drowning and dissolution; it is also an initiation into the deep mysteries of the archetypal psyche. And every depth experience that one lives through consistently has these opposite aspects. On the one hand, one is in fear of perishing, and on the other hand, things are being revealed that one doesn't dare think or speak about.

I must mention in this regard another of those beautiful Jewish legends which illustrates the ambiguous meaning of the symbol of the depths. It concerns the Jonah story. In the Biblical account, Jonah, because he refused to obey God's call, was unceremoniously dumped into the sea and then swallowed by the whale. He called to Yahweh from the depths, from the depths of the whale's belly. He repented and then was released. (Jon. 1-2)

But according to the legend, it happened a little differently. When Jonah landed inside the belly of the whale, God graciously took him on an excursion of the mysteries of the universe. He saw all the sights of the divine regions—the lower regions and the upper regions.[94] You see, that gives a whole different perspective than the one implied in the Biblical story. It's the descent into the depths—the positive aspects of it—as an experience of initiation. That is the point Jung is making: the image of the depths has that double aspect. It comes out in alchemy, and one can also see it directly in its psychological application.

One further legend gives us yet another angle to Jonah's story. According to this legend, when Jonah arrived in the belly of the whale he set up residence—it was very commodious and he was very comfortable. In fact, he said it was as comfortable as the inside of a synagogue. (I tell you, these legends go right to the point! Collective religious containment, you see.) Anyway, it was so comfortable that it didn't serve God's purposes. Therefore God had to appoint a second whale to swallow up the first whale—one which had a much smaller belly and also a lot of little fishes already inhabiting it. So things got too cramped for Jonah, and he was forced to repent.[95]

Psalm 103
God as a Loving Father

Before we look at this Psalm, let me say that I have been wondering how I could more effectively convey to you the numinous presence in these texts. The good thing about encountering them in a church setting is all the paraphernalia that speaks to the unconscious. One has made the pilgrimage to the church, is prepared for it, and so it goes in deeper. It's a whole different thing.

But we can't do that. It's as though the modern ego isn't permitted that kind of experience—that's my view of it. The time has now come (at least for those in the psychological vanguard) to have the experience of the *numinosum* individually. That being so, experiencing it collectively is actually interdicted—because collective experience promotes *participation mystique*,[96] which is actually deleterious to the individual experience. So in that sense we are not really permitted to evoke the full intensity of the *numinosum* here because it would be a violation of our individual boundaries.

That said, let's look at Psalm 103.

1. Bless the LORD, O my soul: and all that is within me, bless his holy name.

2. Bless the LORD, O my soul, and forget not all his benefits:

3. Who forgiveth all thine iniquities; who healeth all thy diseases;

4. Who redeemeth thy life from destruction; who crowneth thee with loving kindness and tender mercies;

5. Who satisfieth thy mouth with good things; so that thy youth is renewed like the eagle's.

6. The LORD executeth righteousness and judgment for all that are oppressed.

7. He made known his ways unto Moses, his acts unto the children of Israel.

8. The LORD is merciful and gracious, slow to anger, and plenteous in mercy.

9. He will not always chide: neither will he keep his anger for ever.

10. He hath not dealt with us after our sins; nor rewarded us according to our iniquities.

11. For as the heaven is high above the earth, so great is his mercy toward them that fear him.

12. As far as the east is from the west, so far hath he removed our transgressions from us.

13. Like as a father pitieth his children, so the LORD pitieth them that fear him.

14. For he knoweth our frame; he remembereth that we are dust.

15. As for man, his days are as grass: as a flower of the field, so he flourisheth.

16. For the wind passeth over it, and it is gone; and the place thereof shall know it no more.

17. But the mercy of the LORD is from everlasting to everlasting upon them that fear him, and his righteousness unto children's children;

18. To such as keep his covenant, and to those that remember his commandments to do them.

19. The LORD hath prepared his throne in the heavens; and his kingdom ruleth over all.

20. Bless the LORD, ye his angels, that excel in strength, that do his commandments, hearkening unto the voice of his word.

21. Bless ye the LORD, all ye his hosts; ye ministers of his, that do his pleasure.

22. Bless the LORD, all his works in all places of his dominion: bless the LORD, O my soul.

The central theme here is the image of Yahweh as a loving father. This idea is also mentioned in other places. In Psalm 68:5, for instance, Yahweh is described as "a father of the fatherless." But in the Old Testament as a whole, the image of God as a father is used only a very few times—and even then it refers to the nation of Israel, not to individuals. One exception is the well-known reference in Proverbs 3:12 which reads: "For whom the LORD loveth he correcteth; even as a father the son in whom he delighteth." A more typical Old Testament reference is Jeremiah 31:9:

> They shall come with weeping, and with supplications will I lead them: I will cause them to walk by the rivers of waters in a straight way, wherein they shall not stumble: for I am a father to Israel, and Ephraim is my first-born. [Ephraim is synonymous with Israel.]

So it turns out that Psalm 103 does have something unique about it: it is really the first time the image of God comes out unequivocally as a loving father. As you know, this theme of God as a loving father is greatly elaborated by Christ. Let me give you an example of that line of thinking as it was developed in the New Testament. Here are two passages from Matthew to give you a flavor of how one would live if one were totally identified with the idea of God as a loving father:

> I am telling you not to worry about your life and what you are to eat, nor about your body and how you are to clothe it. Surely life means more than food, and the body more than clothing! Look at the birds in the sky. They do not sow or reap or gather into barns; yet your heavenly Father feeds them. Are you not worth much more than they are? Can any of you, for all his worrying, add one single cubit to his span of life? And why worry about clothing? Think of the flowers growing in the fields; they never have to work or spin; yet I assure you that not even Solomon in all his regalia [let's say "glory"] was robed like one of these. Now if that is how God clothes the grass in the field which is there today and thrown into the furnace tomorrow, will he not much more look after you, you men of little faith? So do not worry; do not say, "What are we to eat? What are we to drink? How are we to be clothed?" It is the pagans who set their hearts on all these things. Your heavenly Father knows you need them all. Set your hearts on his kingdom first, and on his righteousness, and all these other things will be given you as well. So do not worry about tomorrow: tomorrow will take care of itself. Each day has enough trouble of its own. (Matt. 6:25-34, Jerusalem Bible)

> Ask, and it will be given to you; search, and you will find; knock, and the door will be opened to you. For the one who asks always receives; the one who searches always finds; the one who knocks will always have the door opened to him. Is there a man among you who would hand his son a

stone when he asked for bread? Or would hand him a snake when he asked for a fish? If you, then, who are evil, know how to give your children what is good, how much more will your Father in heaven give good things to those who ask him! (Matt. 7:7-11, Jerusalem Bible)

Well, that lays it out. Trouble is, who believes it? Certainly the loving father is an authentic and genuine aspect of the experience of the Self. That is indisputable—but only sometimes. Once the ego has done all in its power to meet and fulfill its own needs, then it is likely that the loving father aspect of the Self will manifest. But there is no way of determining by external means when that point has been reached. We can only know that by the inner material, by what emerges from the unconscious. It does come up in dreams on certain occasions—usually in times of urgent ego-need. Then it can truly be said, "Blessed are the poor in spirit: for theirs is the kingdom of heaven." (Matt. 5:3) In that respect it's very similar to the Good Shepherd aspect of the Self—they overlap there—and then it brings its healing and rejuvenating effect. But it can't be taken as an accurate description of the totality of the Self.

Comment from the audience: It seems to me that some Jungians idealize and romanticize the unconscious at the cost of disparaging or undervaluing the ego, with the idea that you can trust yourself to the unconscious, put yourself in the arms of your dreams and everything will be lovely. It seems to me that that is not Jung's attitude. If you have a problem, you do your damnedest on the conscious level, and then pray, or have a dream, or look for help.

Edinger: Well, I agree with that, and it goes along with what I have been saying. I think what happens is that innocent and naive egos will be dependent on parental functioning wherever they can find it, and one's relation to the unconscious will be determined by one's immature attitude toward life. You may think of the unconscious as a loving parent who will take care of you. But, sooner or later, experience is apt to contradict that naive assumption. On the other hand, every individual has his or her own proper level of being. If you have reached whatever your limit is, and have found a suitable collective container for it, then you can get away with innocent immaturity. As I see it, that is what churches and collective containments of various kinds are for. We each must find our own appropriate level.

Comment from the audience: It seems to me that the Christian myth is more polarizing than the Jewish one. In the Judaic Scriptures you don't find the extremes; they seem to take the opposites as they exist with more willingness than does the Christian myth.

Edinger: That's true. It's one of the differences. Christian psychology is dissociated psychology. Heaven and earth are split apart. But remember that the opposites must be separated if consciousness is to develop.

You see, from the psychological standpoint all religious symbol systems are various externalized embodiments of the archetypal psyche. Different systems have different emphases, but what the images express always comes ultimately from the psyche. So these splits, these opposites that are emphasized more in one place than another, they all come from the psyche. And when they return to the psyche, then the psyche becomes the major thing, and the various religious formulations become interesting and important illustrations of the reality of the psyche. But if one is contained within a given religious dogmatic structure, then the psyche as such cannot be perceived. The religion fills up all the space and only the religion exists. As long as that works for an individual, one is spared the direct experience of the psyche. The reality of the psyche as such cannot be experienced in such a situation.

I'd like to speak about another image that comes up in Psalm 103: the kingdom of God, or the kingdom of heaven. Verse 19 says "The LORD hath prepared his throne in the heavens; and his kingdom ruleth over all." This, again, is an image that shows up in various places in the Old Testament.[97] The chief reference is in Psalm 145:13 which reads: "Thy kingdom is an everlasting kingdom and thy dominion endureth throughout all generations." Other translations are *basileia panton ton aionon,*[98] "kingdom of all ages" (Septuagint); *regnum omnium saeculorum,* "kingdom for all ages" (Vulgate);

"Your sovereignty is an eternal sovereignty" (Jerusalem Bible); and the literal Hebrew, "a kingdom of all eternities."

The kingdom of God, of heaven, appears in Kabbalistic symbolism as Malchuth, the tenth Sephirot of the Sephirotic Tree (Figure 13). She is the Kingdom of Heaven, the Knesset Ysreal (Community of Israel), the Shekinah (Divine Presence), Moon, Mother and Bride.[99]

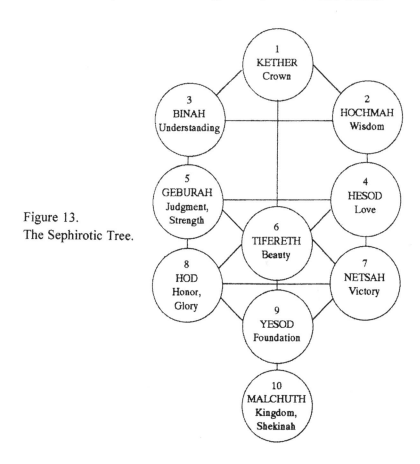

Figure 13.
The Sephirotic Tree.

The image of the kingdom of God received a lot of elaboration in the New Testament. The kingdom of God or the kingdom of heaven is what is prayed for in the Lord's Prayer. Two central themes of the Lord's Prayer are God as a loving father and the kingdom of heaven:

"Our Father who art in heaven, hallowed be thy name. Thy kingdom come, thy will be done on earth, as it is in heaven. Give us this day our daily bread." (Matt. 6:9-11) As a father gives his children bread.

The basic psychological idea expressed here is a request for the Self to take over the rule of the psyche: "Thy kingdom come." But, you know, the ordinary person praying that prayer doesn't have the slightest idea what he's asking for. He really doesn't, because, although the prayer belongs to the loving father image of the Self, as I've said, it is only part of the picture, not the totality—it leaves out the dark side of the Self.

There's another interesting image in here that I want to talk about, especially because it gives me an excuse to quote Augustine again, and I enjoy doing that because I see so many psychological references in his work. Verse 5 of Psalm 103 reads: "Who satisfieth thy mouth with good things; so that thy youth is renewed like the eagle's." That's the phrase: "Thy youth is renewed like the eagle's."

First, let us see what *Physiologus* says of the eagle:

> When he grows old, his wings grow heavy and his eyes grow dim. What does he do then? He seeks out a fountain and then flies up into the atmosphere of the sun, and he burns away his wings and the dimness of his eyes, and descends into the fountain and bathes himself three times and is restored and made new again.
>
> Therefore, you also, if you have the old clothing and the eyes of your heart have grown dim, seek out the spiritual fountain who is the Lord. "They have forsaken me; the fountain of living water" [Jer. 2:13]. As you fly into the height of the sun of justice [Mal. 4:2], who is Christ as the Apostle says, he himself will burn off your old clothing which is the devil's. Therefore, those two elders in Daniel heard, "You have grown old in wicked days" [Dan. 13:52]. Be baptized in the everlasting fountain, putting off the old man and his actions and putting on the new, you who have been created after the likeness of God [cf. Eph. 4:24] as the Apostle said. Therefore David said, "Your youth will be renewed like the eagle's" [Ps. 103:5].[100]

Well, that's an overlap with the phoenix myth.[101] When the eagle grows old, it has to go through a process of rejuvenation. And here's what Augustine has to say about that. As I'm reading this, ask yourself what this would mean psychologically, because that is our concern.

> The eagle is said, after it becometh overpowered with bodily age, to be incapable of taking food from the immoderate length of its beak, which is always increasing. For after the upper part of its beak, which forms a crook above the lower part, hath increased from old age to an immoderate length, the length of this increase will not allow of its opening its mouth, . . . For unless there be such an opening, it hath no power of biting like a forceps, by which to shear off what it may put within its jaws. The upper part therefore increasing, and being too far hooked over, it cannot open its mouth, and take any food. This old age doth to it, it is weighed down with the infirmity of age, and becometh too weak from want of power to eat; . . . By a natural device, therefore, in order in some measure to restore its youth, the eagle is said to dash and strike against a rock the upper lip of its beak, by the too great increase of which the opening for eating is closed: and by thus rubbing it against the rock, it breaketh off the weight of its old beak, . . . It cometh to its food, and everything is restored: it will be after its old age like a young eagle; the vigour of all its limbs returneth, the lustre of its plumage, the guidance of its wings, it flieth aloft as before, a sort of resurrection taketh place in it.[102]

Now Augustine gets to his moral:

> For this is the object of the similitude, like that of the Moon, which after waning and being apparently intercepted, again is renewed, and becometh full; and signifieth to us the resurrection; but when it is full it doth not remain so; again it waneth, that the signification may never cease. Thus also what hath here been said of the eagle: the eagle is not restored unto immortality, but we are unto eternal life; but the similitude is derived from hence, that the rock taketh away from us what hindereth us. Presume not therefore on thy strength: the firmness of the rock rubbeth off thy old age: for that Rock was Christ. In Christ our youth shall be restored like that of the eagle.[103]

It is very interesting to me how Augustine's fantasy plays on this imagery and always ends up back with Christ. That's because Christ is the center of his being, just as the alchemists' fantasy always ends up with the Philosophers' Stone because that is the center of their being.

And the Jungian fantasy always ends with the Self because that is the center of our model of the nature of the psyche. But we can easily interpret what Augustine is talking about in our own psychological terms.

The beak of the eagle is the ego overgrown by accrescenses. It has to be chipped away by being hit against the rock and—without going into all the symbolism of the rock—the rock is a symbol of the Self. The *lapis* is a rock; Christ is a rock. That's what this Psalm says, you see. "My youth is renewed like the eagle's." But Augustine's fantasy implies that renewal is not utterly comfortable; it has traumatic aspects. If you have to hit your beak against a rock in order to be renewed, you see, it does bring another perspective to it.

Figure 14. Eagle Chipping Away at a Rock.
(Woodcut in the 1587 edition of *Physiologus;* Newberry Library, Chicago)

Psalm 110
The Messiah, King and Priest

1. The LORD said unto my Lord, Sit thou at my right hand, until I make thine enemies thy footstool.

2. The LORD shall send the rod of thy strength out of Zion: rule thou in the midst of thine enemies.

3. Thy people shall be willing in the day of thy power, in the beauties of holiness from the womb of the morning: thou hast the dew of thy youth.

4. The LORD hath sworn, and will not repent, Thou art a priest for ever after the order of Melchizedek.

5. The Lord at thy right hand shall strike through kings in the day of his wrath.

6. He shall judge among the heathen, he shall fill the places with the dead bodies; he shall wound the heads over many countries.

7. He shall drink of the brook in the way: therefore shall he lift up the head.

I'm going to read you the Jerusalem Bible version also, to give you another slant. It's short enough to allow that.

Yahweh's oracle to you, my Lord, "Sit at my right hand
and I will make your enemies a footstool for you."

Yahweh will force all your enemies
under the sway of your sceptre in Zion.

Royal dignity was yours from the day you were born,
   on the holy mountains,
royal from the womb, from the dawn of your earliest days.

Yahweh has sworn an oath which he never will retract,
"You are a priest of the order of Melchizedek, and for ever."

The Lord is at your right hand.
When he grows angry he shatters kings,
he gives the nations their deserts,
smashing their skulls, he heaps the wide world with corpses.

Drinking from the stream as he goes,
he can hold his head high in victory.

This is one of the major Messianic Psalms. It is taken by Jews to refer to the coming of the Messiah, and Christians take it to refer to Christ. A footnote in the Jerusalem Bible says about this:

> The prerogatives of the Messiah, worldwide sovereignty and perpetual priesthood, cf. 2 S 7:1+; Zc 6:12-13, are no more conferred by earthly investiture than were those of the mysterious Melchizedek, Gn 14:18+. V. 1 is accepted in the N.T. epistles and elsewhere as a prophecy of the ascension of Christ to the right hand of the Father.[104]

This is the third Messianic Psalm we've talked about. Let me say a word or two about how I understand the image of the Messiah psychologically. I see it as representing the realized, manifested or actualized Self. Up to now this image has taken two forms. In the Jewish version it's projected into future history—the Messiah-to-be. There are marvelous symbolic images associated with this in the legends about the Messianic age—what will happen when the Messiah comes—and they are individuation images.[105]

In the second version, the Christian one, the Messiah image is projected onto Christ. According to that version, the Messiah has already come—but there's a wavering there because he is going to come again. He came the first time, and he will come a second time. So the second time ties in with the Jewish projection. To the extent that he is pictured as having already come, then what you have is a kind of reification of the Messiah image which embeds him in a religious framework carried by a church. It remains projected, this time in a collective metaphysical formulation; the image is not yet available for individual experience—it still has to be related to in projection.

But the psychological approach changes that. Let me remind you that my aim is to pry these images out of their metaphysical, creedal context and apply them to the individual's experience of the psyche. Thus the attributes of "worldwide sovereignty and perpetual priesthood" become part of the phenomenology of the Self—no longer projected into the future Messiah as in the Judaic tradition, or projected into Christ as in the Christian one. The psychological approach sees the image of the Messiah as an image of the Self which can be encountered in the process of individuation.

So this Psalm tells us that the realized or actualized Self—the Messiah—has the attributes of worldwide sovereignty and perpetual priesthood. Now let's pursue this a little further.

Verse 1 says: "The LORD said unto my Lord" (Yahweh said unto the Messiah—that's the translation: "my Lord" is the Messiah; "the LORD" is Yahweh). Yahweh said unto the Messiah, "Sit thou at my right hand, until I make thine enemies thy footstool." Christ refers to this very verse in his disputation with the Pharisees:

> While the Pharisees were gathered round, Jesus put to them this question, "What is your opinion about the Christ [the Messiah]? Whose son is he?" "David's," they told him. "Then how is it," he said, "that David, moved by the Spirit, calls him Lord, where he says:
>
> > *The LORD said to my Lord:*
> > *Sit at my right hand*
> > *and I will put your enemies*
> > *under your feet?*
>
> "If David can call him Lord, then how can he be his [David's] son?" Not one could think of anything to say in reply, and from that day no one dared to ask him any further questions. (Matt. 22: 41-46, Jerusalem Bible)

Now I'm going to answer that question. You see, the question is how can the Messiah be both son of an empirical, historical man—David—and also be his Lord? This can only be understood psychologically, because it refers to the paradoxical relation of the ego to the realized Self. You remember, I defined the Messiah as the realized or actualized Self. The realized Self is, in part at least, the son of the ego. And at the same time it's the superordinate authority and Lord *over* the ego. That's the paradox.

The same issue came up when we talked about the term "son of man" which is a synonym for the Messiah.[106] Christ applied that term to himself, and it comes up in an expression of the alchemists: one of the synonyms for the Philosophers' Stone is *filius philosophorum,* the son of the philosophers. In other words, the Philosophers' Stone is the son of the alchemist who managed to create it. And the psychological point is that the actualized Self is the son—the result—of the devoted efforts of the ego to bring it into conscious existence. So it is legitimate to speak of the Self in one aspect—the actualized aspect—as the son of the ego. Paradoxical, and yet it fits the psychological material. It's an accurate description of the way things are.[107]

I want to consider the phrase in verse 4: "Thou art a priest for ever after the order of Melchizedek." That is one of the aspects of the Messiah as described here, and refers to the 14th chapter of Genesis. There, Abram[108] pursues a marauding band which had taken his nephew Lot captive. He defeats the marauders, rescues Lot and the captured goods. Then the account continues:

> When Abram came back after. . . [defeating the marauders] . . . . Melchizedek king of Salem brought bread and wine; he was a priest of God Most High. He pronounced this blessing:
>
> "Blessed be Abram by God Most High, creator of heaven and earth, and blessed be God Most High for handing over your enemies to you."
>
> And Abram gave him a tithe of everything. (Gen. 14:17-20, Jerusalem Bible)

Let me read you a footnote from the Jerusalem Bible here, because it summarizes concisely a whole body of thinking about this figure of Melchizedek:

> Melchizedek makes a brief and mysterious appearance in the narrative; he is king of that Jerusalem where Yahweh will deign to dwell, and a priest of the Most High even before the levitical priesthood was established; moreover, he receives tithes from the Father of the chosen people [Abraham]. Ps 110:4 represents him as a figure of the Messiah who is both king and priest; the application to Christ's priesthood is worked out in Heb 7. Patristic tradition has developed and enriched this allegorical interpretation: in the bread and wine offered to Abraham it sees an image of the Eucharist and even a foreshadowing of the Eucharistic sacrifice—an interpretation that has been received into the Canon of the Mass. Several of the Fathers even held the opinion that Melchizedek was a manifestation of the Son of God in person. (Gen. 14, fn. g, Jerusalem Bible)

What's so beautiful about working with this material is that it's like examining a rich tapestry that has been woven over a period of many centuries. So you have, for instance, this figure of Melchizedek who shows up in the very early text of Genesis. It has to be derived from somewhere around 1000 B.C.—it may have been written down later, but this image comes from that time. Then it becomes incorporated in the Psalms, written much later. It then emerges as an issue in the New Testament material (Hebrews in particular) and after that, the Patristic Fathers work on it. The result is this great tapestry with threads that extend over a millennium or more, a beautiful image of how the collective psyche reveals itself through the minds of countless individuals over time. And today we see how that panorama of interwoven imagery applies to the empirical psyche as we are privileged to study it in modern terms.

Melchizedek offered Abraham bread and wine. That's all it says. You see, the idea here is that Melchizedek is a priest-king; he is king of Salem and he is also a functioning priest. He is a figure who existed before these two functions had been separated. That makes him very early, because it was very early in human culture that the functions of king and priest were separated. He was a priest prior to the establishment of the levitical priesthood.

So what will this suggest psychologically? It suggests that Melchizedek is an original inner authority whose function is applicable to both the outer world (as king) and the inner world (as priest) simultaneously—before the separation of the opposites, and before the setting up of collective religious procedures. The Psalm is saying, then, that the coming Messiah will be a return to that original whole represented by Melchizedek, and therefore his sovereignty will simultaneously pertain to the outer and inner worlds. It will be a union, a consolidation: a return to the original state of wholeness—but on a conscious, realized level.

Now the Letter to the Hebrews in the New Testament, which at one time was attributed to Paul, equates Melchizedek with Christ. Let me read some of that. It is part of the tapestry I'm talking about.

> You remember that Melchizedek, king of Salem, a priest of God Most
> High, went to meet Abraham who was on his way back after defeating the

kings, and blessed him; and also that it was to him that Abraham gave a tenth of all that he had. By the interpretation of his name [i.e., the meaning of the word "Melchizedek"], he is, first, "king of righteousness" and also king of Salem, that is, "king of peace"; he has no father, mother or ancestry, and his life has no beginning or ending; he is like the Son of God. He remains a priest for ever.

Now think how great this man must have been, if the patriarch Abraham paid him a tenth of the treasure he had captured. We know that any of the descendants of Levi who are admitted to the priesthood are obliged by the Law to take tithes from the people, and this is taking them from their own brothers although they too are descended from Abraham. But this man, who was not of the same descent, took his tenth from Abraham, and he gave his blessing to the holder of the promises.

(Heb. 7:1-6, Jerusalem Bible)

You know, I don't think we can appreciate in what high regard Abraham was held by the ancient Jews. He was above Moses. And to be a descendant of Abraham—Abraham was the original holder of the promise of Yahweh! That's what's being expressed here. The author of Hebrews, wide-eyed, is saying "Melchizedek took tithes from Abraham! What kind of greatness he must represent!" The passage continues:

Now it is indisputable that a blessing is given by a superior to an inferior. Further, in the one case it is ordinary mortal men who receive the tithes, and in the other, someone who is declared to be still alive. It could be said that Levi himself, who receives tithes, actually paid them, in the person of Abraham, because he was still in the loins of his ancestor when *Melchizedek came to meet him.* (Heb. 7:7-10, Jerusalem Bible)

So this is all part of identifying Christ with Melchizedek, you see. And it's particularly interesting that we're told "Melchizedek has no father, mother, or ancestry, and his life has no beginning or ending." Well, where did the author of Hebrews get such an idea? He's talking mythologically—how else? That happens so often in the Scriptures. At times they are written out of a semi-somnambulistic state in which the unconscious speaks directly. "He has no father, mother or ancestry, and his life has no beginning or ending." That's what we're told.

But what it speaks of, then, is that Melchizedek is an archetypal image that exists prior to and beyond ego-consciousness, because ego-consciousness is finite and limited to the categories of time and space. An entity with no beginning and no ending, no father or mother or ancestry—that's an archetype. That's what Melchizedek is.

You see, there was tremendous respect for the levitical priesthood at the time this was written. And what the author of Hebrews says is that the levitical priesthood didn't even exist yet—Levi was still in the loins of Abraham. But the levitical priesthood, in effect, paid tithes to Melchizedek through the person of Abraham, their ancestor. The writer is wondering what a superior figure Melchizedek is that he could even oblige the not-yet-existing levitical priesthood to tithe to him. You get it? It establishes Melchizedek as an archetype—part of the phenomenology of the Self—that's the point.

Figure 15. The Meeting of Abraham and Melchizedek.
(Painting by Peter Paul Rubens)

Psalm 126
Sow in Tears, Reap in Joy

1. When the LORD turned again the captivity of Zion, we were like them that dream.

2. Then was our mouth filled with laughter, and our tongue with singing: then said they among the heathen, The LORD hath done great things for them.

3. The LORD hath done great things for us; whereof we are glad.

4. Turn again our captivity, O LORD, as the streams in the south.

5. They that sow in tears shall reap in joy.

6. He that goeth forth and weepeth, bearing precious seed, shall doubtless come again with rejoicing, bringing his sheaves with him.

Here's the same thing in the Jerusalem Bible version:

Song of the returning exiles

When Yahweh brought Zion's captives home,
    at first it seemed like a dream;
then our mouths filled with laughter
    and our lips with song.

Even the pagans started talking
    about the marvels Yahweh had done for us!
What marvels indeed he did for us,
    and how overjoyed we were!

Yahweh, bring all our captives back again
    like torrents in the Negeb!
Those who went sowing in tears
    now sing as they reap.

They went away, went away weeping,
    carrying the seed;
they come back, come back singing,
    carrying their sheaves.

This Psalm refers to the Babylonian Captivity. The Babylonians conquered the southern kingdom of Judah and its capital Jerusalem, and then instigated a series of deportations of the Jews to Babylon. There was one in 597 B.C., the major one in 586 B.C., and another in 581 B.C. But then in 536 B.C. Cyrus the Great of Persia conquered Babylonia and gave permission for the Jews to return to their homeland. That's the historical context of this Psalm.

But, of course, the Babylonian Captivity has taken on a kind of classic symbolic meaning in the Western psyche. And so, as in so many of these Biblical images, it shows up in alchemy. For instance, chapter 8 of *Aurora Consurgens* is titled "Of the Gate of Brass and Bar of Iron of the Babylonian Captivity." This is an alchemical text, I remind you. It speaks of the redemption of the *anima mundi* (the soul of the world) or *Sapientia Dei* (Sophia, the feminine personification of the wisdom of God) from the darkness of matter—the "Babylonian Captivity." For the alchemist, this parallels the alchemical "extraction of the 'fluid soul' from the mineral body (ore or iron)."[109] The extraction is brought about by a liquifaction or *solutio*—and tears are both a cause and an effect of *solutio*.[110]

The image and experience of captivity is one phase of the individuation process. It is part of the whole symbolism of slavery, imprisonment, confinement, chains and constraints of all kinds. One of the features of the ego's initial encounter with the other center of the personality—the Self—is that the ego is subjected to galling limitations. It can no longer do what it wants, so it experiences the Self as a prison. To put it another way, the ego is nailed to the cross of matter, to reality as it actually is.[111] But then, at a subsequent phase, there is a sense of release from captivity, a rescue—which is what this Psalm is expressing, because the ego has had a change of attitude and can accept the limitations the Self has imposed.

Attitudes, you know, are kind of miraculous. Almost all psychological distress derives from the ego's attitude toward a given experience. If the conscious attitude changes—even though circumstances don't—the distress is very largely mitigated. If the ego accepts the limitations which previously had been so galling, then they are no longer experienced as a prison. It is as though the doors have been flung open—you can leave Babylon and go back to Jerusalem.

The experience of the Babylonian Captivity comes up in other parts of the Psalms. For instance, in Psalm 137:1: "By the rivers of Babylon, there we sat down, yea, we wept, when we remembered Zion." There's the sowing of tears. Again in Psalm 56:8: "Thou tellest my wanderings: put thou my tears into thy bottle: are they not in thy book?"

This takes us to the significant verses 5 and 6 of Psalm 126:

They that sow in tears shall reap in joy.
He that goeth forth and weepeth, bearing precious seed, shall doubtless come again with rejoicing, bringing his sheaves with him.

This passage states almost overtly—you don't have to read much into it—that the seeds sown are tears. So the psychological idea, then, would be that tears or sorrow are creative.[112] And that fits in with other mythological data. For instance, according to Egyptian mythology, mankind was created from the tears of the eye of Ra. "The gods I created from my sweat, but mankind is from the tears of mine eye."[113] This eye was thought of as a separate entity, identified with the Great Goddess in her terrible aspect, and sometimes it is her tears that are said to have created mankind.[114]

In other folklore, weeping often accompanied the sowing of grain because it was seen as a burial. As the sowers (who would be women because women were the originators of agriculture) planted the grain, they would bewail the death of the fertility god. They thought that if they grieved sufficiently it would ensure his resurrection in the spring.[115] So this all has to do with *mortificatio* symbolism.[116] Let me just mention a few other particularly relevant examples.

There are pictures from Egypt, for instance, that show stalks of grain sprouting from the dead body of Osiris. Osiris, in one aspect, was the vegetation spirit, and so he went through the annual cycle of death and rebirth. This is a very basic image for all of ancient Egypt's funeral symbolism and for the elaborate transformation mysteries they projected into the afterlife.

Figure 16. Grain Growing from the Grave, Symbolizing Resurrection.
(From A.E. Waite, *The Hermetic Museum*)

In his famous passage concerning the resurrection of the dead, the Apostle Paul uses this seed image deriving from Egyptian material:

> It [meaning the human being] is sown in corruption; it is raised in incorruption: It is sown in dishonour; it is raised in glory: it is sown in weakness; it is raised in power:
> It is sown a natural body; it is raised a spiritual body. (1 Cor. 15:42-44)

Once again, a projection of the psychological transformation mystery into the afterlife. Same way the Egyptians did it.

In a Gnostic text, the Anthropos is called a corpse because he is buried in the body like a mummy in a tomb. And Jung points out that there is a parallel idea in Paracelsus who says: "Life, verily, is naught but a kind of embalmed mummy, which preserves the mortal body from the mortal worms."[117]

I don't know whether I can make this clear, but here is a beautiful example of how the whole alchemical process originated in ancient Egyptian mortuary symbolism. The Egyptians thought that if they could work properly on the mummy they could turn it into an immortal body. And the alchemists thought the same thing: with the correct procedures they could create their immortal Philosophers' Stone. Paracelsus expresses the idea that the eternal life which exists within the organism is a kind of mummy—already embalmed, and therefore eternal. It's a strange image with a bizarre quality to it, as though the outer being is the tomb—the casket—in which the mummy is buried. But the mummy is the inner core or entelechy (seed). It is eternal, and can come into view as it grows out of the death of the corruptible outer shell. This kind of imagery is what lies behind Psalm 126 about sowing in tears and reaping in joy.

Now let's see if I can make this still more psychological. Experience teaches us that psychological encounters with death, loss, grief, with sorrows of all kinds—when consciously met and dealt with—lead to a deepening and enlargement of the personality, to a harvest rather than to a loss. The tears of sorrow are in fact psychological seeds which, when harvested, bring renewal and an increase of life on a new level. That's what this image is all about. And it's psychologically verified when, as happens in the analytic process, one examines and reflects over a considerable period of time upon the experience of sorrow.

Psalm 139
God's Omniscience

This is a long Psalm but, in my opinion, a big one. I will read both versions.

1. O LORD, thou hast searched me, and known me.

2. Thou knowest my downsitting and mine uprising, thou understandest my thought afar off.

3. Thou compassest my path and my lying down, and art acquainted with all my ways.

4. For there is not a word in my tongue, but, lo, O LORD, thou knowest it altogether.

5. Thou has beset me behind and before, and laid thine hand upon me.

6. Such knowledge is too wonderful for me; it is high, I cannot attain unto it.

7. Whither shall I go from thy spirit? or whither shall I flee from thy presence?

8. If I ascend up into heaven, thou art there: if I make my bed in hell, behold, thou art there.

9. If I take the wings of the morning, and dwell in the uttermost parts of the sea;

10. Even there shall thy hand lead me, and thy right hand shall hold me.

11. If I say, Surely the darkness shall cover me; even the night shall be light about me.

12. Yea, the darkness hideth not from thee; but the night shineth as the day: the darkness and the light are both alike to thee.

13. For thou hast possessed my reins [kidneys]: thou hast covered me in my mother's womb.

14. I will praise thee; for I am fearfully and wonderfully made: marvellous are thy works; and that my soul knoweth right well.

15. My substance was not hid from thee, when I was made in secret, and curiously wrought in the lowest parts of the earth.

16. Thine eyes did see my substance, yet being unperfect; and in thy book all my members were written, which in continuance were fashioned, when as yet there was none of them.

17. How precious also are thy thoughts unto me, O God! how great is the sum of them!

18. If I should count them, they are more in number than the sand: when I awake, I am still with thee.

19. Surely thou wilt slay the wicked, O God: depart from me therefore, ye bloody men.

20. For they speak against thee wickedly, and thine enemies take thy name in vain.

21. Do not I hate them, O LORD, that hate thee? and am not I grieved with those that rise up against thee?

22. I hate them with perfect hatred: I count them mine enemies.

23. Search me, O God, and know my heart: try me, and know my thoughts:

24. And see if there be any wicked way in me, and lead me in the way everlasting.

You get the feeling that different levels of expression erupt. Now here's the Jerusalem Bible version:

Yahweh, you examine me and know me,
you know if I am standing or sitting,
you read my thoughts from far away,
whether I walk or lie down, you are watching,
you know every detail of my conduct.

The word is not even on my tongue,
Yahweh, before you know all about it;
close behind and close in front you fence me round,
shielding me with your hand.
Such knowledge is beyond my understanding,
a height to which my mind cannot attain.

Where could I go to escape your spirit?
Where could I flee from your presence?
If I climb the heavens, you are there,

there too, if I lie in Sheol.

If I flew to the point of sunrise,
or westward across the sea,
your hand would still be guiding me,
your right hand holding me.

If I asked darkness to cover me,
and light to become night around me,
that darkness would not be dark to you,
night would be as light as day.

It was you who created my inmost self,
and put me together in my mother's womb;
for all these mysteries I thank you:
for the wonder of myself, for the wonder of your works.

You know me through and through,
from having watched my bones take shape
when I was being formed in secret,
knitted together in the limbo of the womb.

You have scrutinised my every action,
all were recorded in your book,
my days listed and determined,
even before the first of them occurred.

God, how hard it is to grasp your thoughts!
How impossible to count them!
I could no more count them than I could the sand,
and suppose I could, you would still be with me.

God, if only you would kill the wicked!
Men of blood, away from me!
They talk blasphemously about you,
regard your thoughts as nothing.

Yahweh, do I not hate those who hate you,
and loathe those who defy you?
I hate them with a total hatred,
I regard them as my own enemies.

God, examine me and know my heart,
probe me and know my thoughts;

make sure I do not follow pernicious ways
and guide me in the way that is everlasting.

This is quite a magnificent description of the ubiquity of the Self. As verse 16 suggests, it is even present before the organism has been formed: "in thy book all my members were written . . . when as yet there was none of them." It's as though what's being expressed here is the psychological equivalent of the genetic code! And we have empirical reasons to believe that there is such a thing. (In earliest infancy the ego germ is present as a potentiality; only very gradually does it emerge from the Self.)[118] The Self is the totality of the psyche—including the ego—and, simultaneously, the center of it. Larger and more comprehensive than the ego, it encompasses it on all sides, seeing the ego and relating to it from a larger standpoint than the ego can grasp. That is what this Psalm is expressing.

Go where he will, the psalmist is perpetually under the scrutiny of the Eye of God. This is a major aspect of the encounter with the Self, the experience of being an object of scrutiny. I consider this at some length in *The Creation of Consciousness*,[119] but I want to repeat some of that material here because it is so relevant to this Psalm.

Being scrutinized by the Eye of God has to do with the implications and consequences of the original separation of opposites—most importantly, the separation of subject from object. Jung considered this particular antithesis to be of primary importance. It is, in fact, fundamental to his theory of types: the distinction between extravert and introvert has as its basis the conceptual image of the separation of subject and object.[120] In my opinion, the psychological significance and consequences of that separation can hardly be overestimated.

Consciousness is born with the separation of subject and object. Mythologically, as Erich Neumann has elaborated, this corresponds to the separation of the world parents,[121] and it is fundamental to the phenomenon of consciousness and to the existence of the ego. But it is only a partial phenomenon so far as human psychology is concerned. Subject and object are not separated in the unconscious, nor are the opposites. Opposites separate only when they encounter a conscious ego. And no matter how conscious any one of us might be, our consciousness is still limited—there will always be vast areas of the unconscious in which no separation has taken place. And so, throughout an individual's lifetime, the process must be repeated over and over. Each time the ego falls into an unconscious content it can be brought to consciousness only by an act of separation that allows the ego to see the emerging psychic content and thus become disidentified from it.

The original emergence of the individual ego was an incredible event. The subject, the individual glimmering light of conscious being, recognized itself as distinct from what it was looking at. I am I, and that is that! I am looking at that! I am seeing that! When this happened—when it happens now—a great schism takes place in the psyche. The ego separates from the unconscious and a dissociation occurs. Consciousness is based on psychological dissociation—the subject-object dissociation.

Then, as the ego develops, it increasingly establishes itself as the subject, the arbiter of everything. All else is an object to it—even its own body and its own psychological processes are objects. And this process of perception and knowledge is an expression of the sovereignty of the ego. The ego is the eye, the seer. Everybody else and everything else is being seen, the known object. The ego is the sovereign king of knowledge. Until, that is, the astonishing event takes place when, in one form or another, you see an eye looking back at you! And that strikes terror. Suddenly the subject-object antithesis has been reversed. You are no longer the knower in control of the seeing and knowing process. Rather, you are the one who is being looked at, scrutinized. You feel like a butterfly transfixed on a pin. That is the consequence of an encounter with the Self. The Self is that other source of consciousness watching the ego.

You can study your dreams for a long time before the reality of this hits you. You can gain many insights, have all sorts of realizations and say, "My, how wise these dreams are. I would never have thought of that." But then, sooner or later, the question dawns: where do these dreams come from? Whose knowledge is expressed by them? And—if

Figure 17. Dream Image of the Eye of God.
(From Marion Woodman, *The Owl Was a Baker's Daughter*)

you follow up those thoughts—you are led to the Eye of God aspect of the Self. Jung calls it "a moment of deadliest peril!"[122] At that point, the ego is toppled from the sovereign position of being the subject who knows the object and becomes instead the object—the known one—a scrutinized entity that is being seen by another subject. The other subject is the Self. This is what Psalm 139 is about.

Let me give you one idea of how mythology speaks of this experience. This comes from Egyptian mythology:

> The Eye of the High God is the Great Goddess of the universe in her terrible aspect. Originally it had been sent out into the Primeval Waters by God on an errand to bring back Shu and Tefnut to their father. Thus the Eye is the daughter of the High God. When it returned, it found that it had been supplanted in the Great One's face by another—a surrogate eye—which we can interpret as the sun or moon. This was the primary cause for the wrath of the Eye and the great turning point in the development of the universe, for the Eye can never be fully or permanently appeased. The High God . . . turned it into a rearing cobra, which he bound around his forehead to ward off his enemies [Figure 18, next page].[123]

There's another aspect of the Eye of God:

> Re, the god who created himself, was originally king over gods and men together, but mankind schemed against his sovereignty, for he began to grow old . . . .When he realized that mankind was plotting against him he said to . . . [the other gods]: "Go, summon me hither my Eye. . . ." [And so it was brought forward.] "Behold mankind, who came from my Eye, have been scheming against me. Tell me what you would do about it". . .
>
> Then Nun said: "O Re, my son! O God greater than he who made him and mightier than they who created him! O You that now sit upon your throne! If your Eye were turned against those who are plotting against you, how greatly would they fear you?" . . .
>
> Then the others who were about him said: "Let your Eye be sent out to seize those who are plotting evil against you. . . . Let it descend upon them as Hathor." So that goddess came and slew mankind in the desert.[124]

This kind of imagery gives you an idea of what it feels like to encounter the Eye of God.

Figure 18. Statue of Tutankhamun Showing Cobra Headdress.
(From 1977 Calendar, *The Treasures of Tutankhamun;*
The Metropolitan Museum of Art, New York)

In verse 14 there is a beautiful passage: "I will praise thee, for I am fearfully and wonderfully made." This is an expression of the numinosity of the whole human organism—body and psyche. You know, until the sixteenth century it was absolutely taboo to dissect the human body. There was good reason for that, good psychological reason, because of what is expressed in this verse. The numinosity of the human body was such that it was considered sacrilege to dissect it with the sharp analytic scalpel of the conscious ego. That is the hubris of the modern mind—it has dissected not only the body, but the mind, and everything else in view. This was necessary for ego development, but at the same time, it is truly a sacrilege, so there is real guilt associated with it.

The same thing applies to the psyche—indeed more so. Depth psychology does not yet by any means have universal recognition. Many people actually consider it sacrilegious. I don't know whether they would use that word exactly, but that is the attitude. And it is. It actually *is* sacrilegious! Because we are "fearfully and wonderfully made."

When I read verse 15—"My substance was not hid from thee, when I was made in secret, and curiously wrought in the lowest parts of the earth"—I am reminded of an alchemical motto that circles the center of a diagram picturing the goal of the work (Figure 19, next page). That motto is the key to the whole opus. If you do what that motto tells you to, you've got the alchemical secret; you will have made the Stone. Translated from the Latin the motto says: "Visit the interior of the earth, rectifying, you will find the secret Stone." Here is a clear parallel to verse 15. In other words, the psalmist was made in the same place that the Philosophers' Stone was made—"in the lowest parts of the earth."

The idea is that in order to create the Philosophers' Stone you must visit the lowest parts of the earth—the deepest layers of the unconscious—and the matter that you find there must then be subject to "rectifying." It has to be corrected; it has to undergo transformation. Out of that process comes the secret, the Philosophers' Stone. That, when paralleled with verse 15 in the Psalm, indicates that the creation of the Philosophers' Stone is equivalent to the original creation of

Figure 19. The Principal Symbols of Alchemy.
(From Trismosin, *La Toyson d'or;* 1612)

the individual. They both take place at the same deep level. This leads us to the astonishing conclusion that the alchemist, as he creates the alchemical Stone—the *lapis*—is duplicating the work of the Creator.

Question: Speaking psychologically, in relation to the Self, who are these enemies that the Psalms keep referring to?

Edinger: Well, I haven't gone into that, but now I will. It's a kind of eruption, isn't it? The psalmist is working on a sublime level and then comes a jarring disturbance in verse 19: "Surely thou will slay the wicked, O God: depart from me therefore, ye bloody men." Now what does that mean?

Here's how I understand it: it is as though his experience of the Self is not fully integrated. That means there is some grandiosity and inflation in it. As a consequence, something of the phenomenology of paranoid psychology comes up. The Eye of God is the crucial feature of paranoid psychology, you see. The paranoid experiences himself as being watched in various kinds of delusional ways—almost always critically. But the idea of being watched implies a certain self-importance—one is worth watching! It is an identification with the Self and with the center of the universe. Everything else is focused on him, watching him. In compensation for that grandiose delusion, the unconscious has to attack. And that attack is projected, you see, onto "the wicked," "mine enemies" in the outer world.

Figure 20.
Egyptian Eye of God.

Psalm 150
Praise the Lord

I feel I know a little something about the Psalms I've talked about so far, but with Psalm 150 I must confess I do not know what I'm talking about experientially. I could have chosen another Psalm to discuss and left this one out, but I didn't feel that was the right thing to do. I started with Psalm 1 and I want to end with Psalm 150. This final Psalm is one of a series of five that have exactly the same content; the final statement of the Psalms is really one line—"Praise ye the LORD"—underscored five times. In view of that, how could I omit it? So I'll read it and give you some thoughts about it—but my thoughts are not based on the same degree of experience as is everything else I have said. It's a brief Psalm so I'm going to read it in both versions.

1. Praise ye the LORD. Praise God in his sanctuary: praise him in the firmament of his power.

2. Praise him for his mighty acts: praise him according to his excellent greatness.

3. Praise him with the sound of the trumpet: praise him with the psaltery and harp.

4. Praise him with the timbrel and dance: praise him with stringed instruments and organs.

5. Praise him upon the loud cymbals: praise him upon the high sounding cymbals.

6. Let every thing that hath breath praise the LORD. Praise ye the LORD.

And the Jerusalem Bible translation:

Alleluia!
Praise God in his Temple on earth,
praise him in his temple in heaven,
praise him for his mighty achievements,
praise him for his transcendent greatness!

Praise him with blasts of the trumpet,
praise him with lyre and harp,
praise him with drums and dancing,
praise him with strings and reeds,
praise him with clashing cymbals,
praise him with clanging cymbals!
Let everything that breathes praise Yahweh! Alleluia!

Well, I think you'll agree there's just one idea in this Psalm: the praise of God. Now, all we have to do is to determine what "Praise the Lord" means psychologically! I'm not sure I know, but I'll do a little work on it. The first thing to consider is the etymology. My approach to a mystery is to start with the word that is used to express it. So I'm going to read you a passage from *Nelson's Expository Dictionary of the Old Testament;* it's a fine book for needs of this sort. Here is what it says about the Hebrew word "to praise":

halal, "to praise, celebrate, glory, sing (praise), boast." The meaning "to praise" is actually the meaning of the intensive form of the Hebrew verb *halal,* which in its simple active form means "to boast." . . . The word is found in Ugaritic in the sense of "shouting" and perhaps "jubilation." Found more than 160 times in the Old Testament, *halal* is used for the first time in Gen. 12:15, where it's noted that because of Sarah's great beauty, the princes of Pharaoh "praised" (KJV, "commended") her to Pharaoh.

While *halal* is often used simply to indicate "praise" of people, including the king (2 Chron. 23:12) or the beauty of Absalom (2 Sam. 14:25), the word is usually used in reference to the "praise" of God. Indeed, not only all living things but all created things, including the sun and moon, are called upon "to praise" God (Ps. 148:2-5, 13; 150:1). Typically, such "praise" is called for and expressed in the sanctuary, especially in times of special festivals (Isa. 62:9).

The Hebrew name for the Book of Psalms is simply the equivalent for the word "praises" and is a bit more appropriate than "Psalms," which comes from the Greek and has to do with the accompaniment of singing with a stringed instrument of some sort. . . .

The word *halal* is the source of "Hallelujah," a Hebrew expression of "praise" to God which has been taken over into virtually every language of mankind. The Hebrew "Hallelujah" is generally translated "Praise the Lord!" The Hebrew term is more technically translated "Let us praise Yah," the term "Yah" being a shortened form of "Yahweh."[125]

Well, that's the first leg of our journey in trying to understand the psychological meaning of "Praise the Lord." It gives us a bit of data anyway and enlarges the implications of the term "praise" to include celebrating, glorifying, singing—and boasting!

Now when we consider this concept of praise of God, it becomes very clear that Yahweh, as pictured throughout the Old Testament, has an inordinate need to be praised. Jung notes this fact in "Answer to Job":

> The character thus revealed [i.e., the fact that he's in constant need of praise] fits a personality who can only convince himself that he exists through his relation to an object. Such dependence on the object is absolute when the subject is totally lacking in self-reflection and therefore has no insight into himself. It is as if he existed only by reason of the fact that he has an object which assures him that he is really there.[126]

You see, this is the function that praise serves: it verifies God's existence. The nation of Israel served this purpose for Yahweh. One aspect of the covenant relationship was the commitment to perpetual praise. And if God needs the verification of his existence, wouldn't this be another version of the way man justifies God, which we talked about in relation to Psalm 51?

It is only within the psychological context that remarks of this sort are permissible. And that, of course, is the only context from which I am speaking because it's the only one I know.

I can do this because what is being referred to is not the metaphysical or theological notion of God, but rather the psychological fact of the God-image. This is all psychology. All the images and all the formulations we use must come from our psychological experience, because we don't have anything else. So we have to anthropomorphize these God-images—that's the only way to bring them into the range of human dealings.

Certainly, in our own personal experience, we are thoroughly familiar with the need for affirmation of our being. It is generally recognized in developmental psychology that a child's environment should transmit not only affirmation that it exists but also evidence that he or she is worthy. That is fundamental in psychological experience. And the basic idea is praise. Call it what you want—any kind of considerate attention and affirmation of one's being, in the large sense of the word, is praise.

As an aside, let me offer here the idea that extraverts are probably more dependent on external praise than introverts. I don't mean to say by this that extraverts are more insecure—not at all. But for the introvert, the justification for being is more apt to derive from within, and that can be just as shaky a source as the outside can be for the extravert. Nonetheless, I think the introvert is more likely to look for that affirmation within rather than without.

And what happens if praise is not forthcoming? Just as the ego, at a certain stage, thirsts for the eternal, so the eternal—the unconscious—thirsts for recognition by the ego. The unconscious, when it is constellated, demands attention. If it does not receive conscious consideration, it messes up one's life so that it gets it in some other way.

I am very fond of an anecdote—this will tell you something about me—that concerns a mule trainer who was teaching the art of mule training to a group of apprentice mule trainers. The mule was brought out and the trainer picked up a 2 x 4 plank and swung it as hard as he could, crashing it into the head of the mule. At this, the mule blinked. And the mule trainer said: "This illustrates the primary point in the training of a mule: first you must get his attention."

That is the way the unconscious treats the ego. When it is activated, when it is ready to be praised, when it demands attention—if that attention is not forthcoming, then the 2 x 4 slams into the ego. It might be an accident, an illness, a bad dream; it might be the breakup of a very important relationship. It might be any one of a number of things—but it is 2 x 4 psychology on the part of the unconscious in order to get the attention of the ego.[127]

I think all these matters are somehow relevant to the question of praise of Yahweh, but as I said at the beginning, I don't quite know what I'm talking about; I'm still on the margin. I think it does imply some kind of total unconditional affirmation of life, this praise of Yahweh. What we're dealing with here is the affirmation of God. Now isn't that an approximate equivalent to the affirmation of life in the ultimate sense of the word? I think it is. With my phenomenological approach, what I have to offer you in this regard is not theory but some examples of what certain individuals have said concerning this matter of the praise of God or, in more mundane terms, the affirmation of life. I will give you three examples: Thomas Carlyle, Nietzsche and Jung.

In Carlyle's very interesting essay entitled *Sartor Resartus,* one of his chapter headings is "The Eternal Nay," and another heading is "The Everlasting Yea." In the latter chapter he has this to say:

But the whim we have of Happiness is somewhat thus. By certain valuations, and averages, of our own striking, we come upon some sort of average terrestrial lot; this we fancy belongs to us by nature, and of indefeasible right. It is simple payment of our wages, of our deserts; requires neither thanks nor complaint; only such *overplus* as there may be do we account Happiness; [Happiness is like affirmation, you see. It all has to do with this "eternal yea."] any *deficit* again is Misery. Now consider that we have the valuation of our own deserts ourselves, and what a fund of Self-conceit there is in each of us,—do you wonder that the balance should so often dip the wrong way, and many a Blockhead cry: See there, what a payment; was ever worthy gentleman so used!—I tell thee, Blockhead, it all comes of thy Vanity; of what thou *fanciest* those same deserts of thine to be. Fancy that thou deservest to be hanged (as is most likely), thou wilt feel it happiness to be only shot. . . .

So true is it, what I then say, that *the Fraction of Life can be increased in value not so much by increasing your Numerator as by lessening your Denominator.* Nay, unless my Algebra deceive me, *Unity* itself divided by *Zero* will give *Infinity.* Make thy claim of wages a zero, then; thou hast the world under thy feet. Well did the Wisest of our time write: "It is only with renunciation (*Entsagen*) that Life, properly speaking, can be said to begin."

I asked myself: What is this that, ever since earliest years, thou hast been fretting and fuming, and lamenting and self-tormenting, on account of? Say it in a word: is it not because thou are not HAPPY? Because the Thou (sweet gentleman) is not sufficiently honoured, nourished, soft-bedded, and lovingly cared for? [Not given enough praise, you see.] Foolish soul! What Act of Legislature was there that *thou* shouldst be Happy? A little while ago thou hadst no right to *be* at all. What if thou wert born and predestined not to be Happy, but to be Unhappy! Art thou nothing other than a Vulture, then, that fliest through the Universe seeking after somewhat to *eat*; and shrieking dolefully because carrion enough is not given thee? Close thy *Byron;* open up thy *Goethe.*

. . . I see a glimpse of it! cries he elsewhere: there is in man a HIGHER than Love of Happiness: he can do without Happiness, and instead thereof find Blessedness! Was it not to preach-forth this same HIGHER that sages and martyrs, the Poet and the Priest, in all times, have spoken and suffered; bearing testimony, through life and through death, of the Godlike that is in Man, and how in the Godlike only has he Strength and Freedom? Which God-inspired Doctrine art thou also honoured to be taught; O Heavens! and broken with manifold merciful Afflictions, even till thou become contrite, and learn it! O, thank thy Destiny for these; thankfully bear what yet remain: thou hadst need of them; the Self [that is, the ego] in thee needed to be annihilated. By benignant fever-paroxysms is Life rooting out the deep-seated chronic Disease, and triumphs over Death. On the roaring billows of Time, thou art not engulfed, but borne aloft into the azure of Eternity. Love not Pleasure; love God. This is the EVERLASTING YEA, wherein all contradiction is solved: wherein whoso walks and works, it is well with him.[128]

Well, that's Thomas Carlyle, whom I see grappling manfully with the question. I'm not satisfied with his answer, because it seems to me that what he has done is just give us another equation, the other part of what Yahweh requires, namely that he be loved. And that's what Carlyle says here: so love God; and if you can do that, then that's the everlasting Yea, the affirmation of life, the "Praise the Lord." But he says it so well!

So does Nietzsche. Here is an excerpt from "The Drunken Song" in *Thus Spake Zarathustra*:

You higher men, what do you think? Am I a soothsayer? A dreamer? A drunkard? An interpreter of dreams? A midnight bell? A drop of dew? A haze and fragrance of eternity? Do you not hear it? Do you not smell it? Just now my world became perfect; midnight too is noon; pain too is a joy; curses too are a blessing; night too is a sun—go away or you will learn: a sage too is a fool.

Have you ever said Yes to a single joy? O my friends, then you said Yes too to *all* woe. All things are entangled, ensnared, enamored; if ever you wanted one thing twice, if ever you said, "You please me, happiness! Abide, moment!" then you wanted *all* back. All anew, all eternally, all entangled, ensnared, enamored—oh, then you *loved* the world. Eternal ones, love it eternally and evermore; and to woe too, you say: go, but return! *For all joy wants—eternity.* All joy wants the eternity of all things, wants honey, wants lees, wants drunken midnight, wants tombs, wants tomb-tears' comfort, wants gilded evening glow.

What does joy not want? It is thirstier, more cordial, hungrier, more terrible, more secret than all woe; it wants *itself,* it bites into *itself,* the ring's will strives in it; it wants love, it wants hatred, it is overrich, gives, throws away, begs that one might take it, thanks the taker, it would like to be hated; so rich is joy that it thirsts for woe, for hell, for hatred, for disgrace, for the cripple, for *world*—this world, oh, you know it!

You higher men, for you it longs, joy, the intractable blessed one—for your woe, you failures. All eternal joy longs for failures. For all joy wants itself, hence it also wants agony. O happiness, O pain! Oh, break, heart! You higher men, do learn this, joy wants eternity. Joy wants the eternity of *all* things, *wants deep, wants deep eternity.*[129]

You see why he calls it "The Drunken Song." Sometimes I think Nietzsche deliberately courted inflation in order to fulfill his destiny of expressing something which could only be expressed in that state. This is an example. But there is profound archetypal reality in what he is saying. This is affirmation of life. But who can bear it in a sane state of mind?

Let me conclude with something more sane. This is Jung's affirmation of life in his autobiography. He talks about the illness he had in 1944 and then goes on to say:

After the illness a fruitful period of work began for me. A good many of my principal works were written only then. The insight I had had, or the vision of the end of all things, gave me the courage to undertake new formulations. I no longer attempted to put across my own opinion, but surrendered myself to the current of my thoughts. Thus one problem after the other revealed itself to me and took shape.

Something else, too, came to me from my illness. I might formulate it as an affirmation of things as they are: an unconditional "yes" to that which is, without subjective protests—acceptance of the conditions of existence as I see them and understand them, acceptance of my own nature, as I happen to be. At the beginning of the illness I had the feeling that there was something wrong with my attitude, and that I was to some extent responsible for the mishap. But when one follows the path of individuation, when one lives one's own life, one must take mistakes into the bargain; life would not be complete without them. There is no guarantee —not for a single moment—that we will not fall into error or stumble into deadly peril. We may think there is a sure road. But that would be the road of death. Then nothing happens any longer—at any rate, not the right things. Anyone who takes the sure road is as good as dead.[130]

That passage touches most of the themes that have come up during our discussions of the various Psalms. One might see it as a kind of subdued "Praise the Lord." I don't think it quite meets the criteria, however. Not quite. I think this final image of the Psalms—five times underlined—involves an attitude of total affirmation of existence, fully conscious of the opposites and yet so beyond them that the affirmation is unimpaired by that full realization. It involves a total affirmation of ego and Self and all the tragedy of their interplay. Even though the full reality of evil in all of its depth and breadth is completely perceived, the affirmation is of such an order as to be undamaged by that awareness.

In my humble opinion, no human has reached that level in full consciousness and sanity. I don't think Jung would claim to have either because, in another place, he speaks of his anxious hope that meaning may turn out to preponderate over meaninglessness in the universe.[131] He's not at all sure it will—but he entertains the anxious hope. Well, that doesn't quite sound like the "Praise the Lord" theme of the final Psalms. In my opinion, such a total affirmation can only be understood currently as a far distant goal.

I'm going to end by reading Psalm 150 in the Vulgate Latin. If I could, I'd read it in Hebrew. That would be preferable—but I can't read Hebrew. So I'll read it in Latin:

Laudate Dominum in sanctuario eius,
laudate eum in augusto firmamento eius.
Laudate eum propter grandia opera eius,
laudate eum propter summam majestatem eius.
Laudate eum clangore tubae,
laudate eum psalterio et cithara.
Laudate eum tympano et choro,
laudate eum chordis et organo.
Laudate eum cymbalis sonoris,
laudate eum cymbalis crepitantibus:
omne quod spirat, laudet Dominum! Alleluia.

Figure 21. David Leads a Group of Musicians Praising the Lord.
(From *The Visconti Hours;* National Library, Florence)

Notes

[1] "Answer to Job," *Psychology and Religion,* CW 11, par. 754. (CW refers throughout to *The Collected works of C.G. Jung)*

[2] See Edward F. Edinger, *The Archetype of the Apocalypse: A Jungian Study of the Book of Revelation,* pp. 55ff.

[3] "Answer to Job," *Psychology and Religion,* CW 11, par. 579.

[4] Cited in Adam Nicolson, *God's Secretaries: The Making of the King James Bible,* p. 243.

[5] CW 14, par. 521.

[6] "The *numinosum* is either a quality belonging to a visible object or the influence of an invisible presence that causes a peculiar alteration of consciousness." ("Psychology and Religion," *Psychology and Religion,* CW 11, par. 6)

[7] Artur Weiser, *The Psalms,* pp. 19f.

[8] C.G. Jung, *Letters,* vol. 2, p. 33.

[9] Joseph Gaer, *The Lore of the Old Testament,* p. 221. In a note, Gaer writes that this legend and other similar ones are "all based on the eloquent Psalmic exclamation: "The waters saw You, O God, the waters saw You and were afraid!" (Ps. 77:16)

[10] The Vulgate is St. Jerome's translation of the Greek and Hebrew sources, started in A.D. 382.

[11] [All Biblical passages are from the Authorized King James Version, unless otherwise noted.—Ed.]

[12] Adam Clarke (1844), quoted in C.H. Spurgeon, *Treasury of David,* 1a, p. 4.

[13] Babylonian Talmud Tract Sabboth (B. Shabb. 89a). Quoted in Raphael Patai, *Gates to the Old City,* pp. 197f. [There is also a version of this legend in Louis Ginsberg, *Legends of the Bible,* p. 397.—Ed.]

[14] [See the beautiful passages from Proverbs and Ecclesiasticus, quoted in "Answer to Job," *Psychology and Religion,* CW 11, pars. 609ff.—Ed.]

[15] CW 14, par. 624.

[16] *Memories, Dreams, Reflections,* p. 176.

[17] "The Philosophical Tree," *Alchemical Studies,* CW 13, par. 350.

[18] Ibid., par. 304: "If a mandala may be described as a symbol of the Self seen in cross-section, then the tree would represent a profile view of it . . . as a process of growth."

[19] Ecclus. 24 (quoted in "Answer to Job," *Psychology and Religion,* CW 11, par. 610).

[20] *Katha Upanishad,* II, 6,1 (quoted in *Mysterium Coniunctionis,* CW 14, par. 158, note 211, and in Edinger, *The Mysterium Lectures,* p. 74).

21 Quoted in "The Philosophical Tree," *Alchemical Studies,* CW 13, par. 412.

22 Augustine, *Exposition on the Book of Psalms,* p. 2.

23 Spurgeon, *Treasury of David,* Ia, p. 8.

24 [See Edinger, *Archetype of the Apocalypse,* especially chap. 9, pp. 147ff.—Ed.]

25 [See Edinger, *Mysterium Lectures,* p. 32.—Ed.]

26 Matt. 7:23: "And then I will profess unto them, I never knew you: depart from me, ye that work iniquity."

27 See Edinger, *The Creation of Consciousness: Jung's Myth for Modern Man,* esp. chap. 2, "The Meaning of Consciousness."

28 See Raphael Patai, *The Messiah Texts,* pp. 165f.

29 Jaroslav Pelikan, *A History of the Development of Doctrine,* vol. 1, p. 175.

30 Jung: "The experience of the Self is always a defeat for the ego." (*Mysterium Coniunctionis,* CW 14, par. 778)

31 *Memories, Dreams, Reflections,* pp. 242ff.

32 Ibid., p. 227.

33 Jane Harrison, *Prolegomena to the Study of Greek Religion,* pp. 573ff., 583, 585 (modified).

34 [Edinger discusses the term "son of man" in several of his books. See especially *Transformation of the God-Image: An Elucidation of Jung's* Answer to Job, chap. 8, where he also goes into the Book of Enoch in some detail.—Ed.]

35 Spurgeon, *Treasury of David,* 1a, 89.

36 [See Edinger, *The Psyche in Antiquity, Book Two: Gnosticism and Early Christianity,* pp. 129ff., for a more extensive commentary on Augustine.—Ed.]

37 Augustine, *Expositions on the Book of Psalms,* p. 30.

38 *Psychology and Religion,* CW 11, par. 675.

39 "Essay on Man," in W.H. Auden and Norman Holmes Pearson, eds., *Poets of the English Language,* vol. 3, p. 395.

40 Jung, *Letters,* vol. 2, p. 314. [See also Edinger, *The New God-Image: A Study of Jung's Key Letters Concerning the Evolution of the Western God-Image,* pp. 77ff., 166ff.—Ed.]

41 Emma Jung and Marie-Louise von Franz, *The Grail Legend,* pp. 51, 295. [See also Richard Wilhelm, trans., *The I Ching or Book of Changes,* Hexagram 4, fn. 1, p. 20.—Ed.]

42 Edinger, *Ego and Archetype: Individuation and the Religious Function of the Psyche,* pp. 38ff.

43 See also Eph. 2:2,3; Rom. 5:12. Other references in the Psalms: 51:5; 58:3; 143:2.

44 Isa. 14:12-14: "... O Lucifer, son of the morning! ... For thou has said in thine heart, I will ascend into heaven, I will exalt my throne above the stars of God: I will sit also upon the mount of the congregation, in the sides of the north: I will ascend above the heights of the clouds; I will be like the most High."

45 [Handel uses this text, as well as passages from Psalm 22, in his great oratorio, The Messiah. For an excellent collection of the Suffering Servant legendary material, see Patai, *The Messiah Texts.*—Ed.]

46 *Physiologus,* pp. 13f.

47 See, for instance, Louis Charbonneau-Lassay, *The Bestiary of Christ,* p. 446.

48 [For further discussion of the symbolic cluster of phoenix, worm and Christ, see Edinger, *Mysterium Lectures,* pp. 212ff.—Ed.]

49 A.E. Waite, trans., *The Hermetic Museum,* vol. 1, pp. 101ff. Extended text in *Mysterium Coniunctionis,* CW 14, par. 485. [Also quoted in Edinger, *Anatomy of the Psyche,* p. 175.—Ed.]

50 [See Edinger, *Anatomy of the Psyche,* chap. 6, "Mortificatio."—Ed.]

51 Adler, "Aspects of Jung's Personality and Work," in *Psychological Perspectives,* Spring 1975, p. 13. [Also quoted in Edinger, *Anatomy of the Psyche,* p. 177.—Ed.]

52 [See Edinger, *Antomy of the Psyche,* chap. 5, "Sublimatio."—Ed.]

53 Jung's footnote here: "Who, *nota bene,* is not to be confused with the ego."

54 CW 14, par. 492.

55 [The Anthropos refers to the original or primordial man, an archeypal image of wholeness in alchemy, religion and Gnosticism. See *Psychology and Religion,* CW 11, pars. 414, 419.—Ed.]

56 In "Life Thoughts," quoted in Spurgeon, *Treasury of David,* Ia, p. 357.

57 *The Visions Seminars,* p. 19. [Spring edition.—Ed.]

58 [The apostolic father Hermas (second century) was the author of *The Shepherd,* a work instructing Christians in their duties; see *Psychological Types,* CW 6, pars. 381ff.—Ed.]

59 *The Visions Seminars,* pp. 24f. [Spring edition.—Ed.]

60 Ibid., p. 25.

61 Ibid.

62 [Knud Rasmussen (1879-1933), was a Danish explorer and ethnologist who wrote *Across Arctic America* (1927), which has recently been republished. His mother was of Eskimo ancestry. Jung also refers to this book and the journey in *Dream Analysis: Notes of the Seminar given in 1928-1930,* pp. 5ff., and in "The Symbolic Life," *The Symbolic Life,* CW 18, par. 674.—Ed.]

63 *The Visions Seminars.* p. 25. [Spring edition.—Ed.]

64 Augustine, *Expositions on the Book of Psalms,* p. 60.

65 Ibid.

66 [For further discussion of the banquet archetype and the Last Supper, see Edinger, *The Christian Archetype: A Jungian Commentary on the Life of Christ,* chap. 6.—Ed.]

67 Patai, *The Messiah Texts,* chap. 5.

68 *The Symbolic Life,* CW 18, pars. 617ff.

69 Gaer, *Lore of the Old Testament,* p. 225.

70 Ginsberg, *Legends of the Bible,* p. 546.

71 In this legend "for twenty-two years [David] was penitent. Daily he wept a whole hour and ate his 'bread with ashes.' But he had to undergo still heavier penance. For a half-year he suffered with leprosy, and even the Sanhedrin [the supreme Jewish council and highest court of justice], which usually was in close personal attendance upon him, had to leave him. He lived not only in physical but also in spiritual isolation, for the Shekinah departed from him during that time. Of all the punishments, however, inflicted upon David, none was so severe as the rebellion of his own son [Absalom]." (Ibid., p. 547)

72 Augustine, *Expositions on the Book of Psalms,* p. 192.

73 Ibid.

74 [For further discussion see Edinger, *The Bible and the Psyche,* pp. 86ff.—Ed.]

75 FitzGerald's "reputation is largely founded on this poem, so free in rendition as to be virtually an original work, and masterful in its concentration, music, and command of tone." (William Rose Benet, ed., *The Reader's Encyclopedia,* p. 352)

76 Fitzgerald, *The Rubaiyat,* verses LXXX-LXXXI.

77 [See Edinger, *Transformation of the God-Image,* p. 35; also "Answer to Job," *Psychology and Religion,* CW 11, par. 757.—Ed.]

78 [See *Mysterium Coniunctionis,* CW 14, pars. 374ff.; *Psychology and Alchemy,* CW 12, pars. 431ff.; and *The Practice of Psychotherapy,* CW 16, par. 533, note 24. Also Edinger, *Mysterium Lectures,* p. 182.—Ed.]

79 Christopher Wordsworth, cited in Spurgeon, *Treasury of David,* vol. 2a, p. 69.

80 See Edinger, *Ego and Archetype,* pp. 48ff.

81 Augustine, *Expositions on the Book of Psalms,* pp. 258f.

82 "The Waste Land," I, lines 19-24; V, lines 331-346, in *Collected Poems, 1909-1935.*

83 Ralph Waldo Emerson, *Selected Writings,* p. 280.

84 [See, for instance, *Mysterium Coniunctionis,* CW 14, pars. 134ff.; also Edinger, *The Mysterium Lectures,* pp. 95ff.—Ed.]

[85] CW 14, pars. 189ff. [See also Edinger, *Mysterium Lectures*, pp. 124ff.—Ed.]

[86] This is a reference to Isa. 40:3: "The voice of him that crieth in the wilderness" (in the German original, *Ruf der Wuste*), with an allusion, in the German text, also to Jack London's novel *The Call of the Wild.*

[87] [Edinger's literal translation from the German, which differs from that in the Collected Works.—Ed.]

[88] *Mysterium Coniunctionis*, CW 14, pars. 189ff.

[89] "Mandalas," *Archetypes and the Collective Unconscious*, CW 9i, pars. 713ff.

[90] Marie-Louise von Franz, ed., *Aurora Consurgens*, parable vii, p. 133.

[91] See above, p. 86, and note 78.

[92] *Mysterium Coniunctionis*, CW 14, par. 469.

[93] Ibid., par. 470.

[94] See Gaer, *Lore of the Old Testament*, pp. 271f.

[95] Ginzberg, *Legends of the Bible*, pp. 605f.

[96] ["A term derived from anthropology and the study of primitive psychology, denoting a mystical connection, or identity, between subject and object." (Daryl Sharp, *Jung Lexicon: A Primer of Terms and Concepts*, p. 96).—Ed.]

[97] [In the interest of time, Edinger omitted the following material on the kingdom of Yahweh and on Malchuth from his lecture. I have reconstructed it from his handwritten notes.—Ed.]

[98] [See Edinger, *The Aion Lectures: Exploring the Self in C.G. Jung's* Aion, pp. 14ff., where his discussion of the various meanings of the word *aion* has a direct bearing on his remarks here about the kingdom of God.—Ed.]

[99] [For further elaboration, see Edinger, *Mysterium Lectures*, pp. 39ff. Also Jung, *Mysterium Coniunctionis*, CW 14, pars. 18f., 638. I was astonished to find the footprints of the feminine principle and of the *coniunctio* in this material. The idea that the Kingdom of Heaven is a feminine entity has profound ramifications. I feel certain that if Edinger had had time to fill out his notes, he would have led us to alchemy as well, and given us crystal water to drink.—Ed.]

[100] *Physiologus*, pp. 12f.

[101] See above, pp. 59ff.

[102] Augustine, *Expositions on the Book of Psalms*, p. 506.

[103] Ibid.

[104] Jerusalem Bible, Psalm 110, footnote a.

[105] Patai, *The Messiah Texts.*

[106] See above, Psalm 8.

[107] [For further discussion of the son of man, see Edinger, *Transformation of the*

God-Image: p. 90—Ed.]

108 [It is not until Gen. 17:5 that Yahweh changes Abram's name to Abraham: "You shall no longer be called Abram; your name shall be Abraham, for I will make you father of a multitude of nations." See Jerusalem Bible, Gen. 17, fn. d.—Ed.]

109 Von Franz, ed., *Aurora Consurgens,* pp. 261ff.

110 [See Edinger, *Anatomy of the Psyche,* chap. 3, "Solutio."—Ed.]

111 [In "Answer to Job," Jung says: "God is Reality itself." (*Psychology and Religion,* CW 11, par. 631) For commentary on the psychological significance of prison imagery in terms of the "provisional life," see Daryl Sharp, *The Secret Raven: Conflict and Transformation in the Life of Franz Kafka,* pp. 68ff.—Ed.]

112 [See above, Psalm 22, on the creative aspect of misery.—Ed.]

113 R.T. Rundle Clark, *Myth and Symbol in Ancient Egypt,* p. 72.

114 Ibid. p. 185.

115 Ad de Vries, *Dictionary of Symbols and Imagery,* p. 496.

116 [See Edinger, *Anatomy of the Psyche,* chap. 6, "Mortificatio."—Ed.]

117 *Aion,* CW 9ii, par. 334.

118 See Edinger, *Ego and Archetype,* pp. 5ff.

119 [See especially chap. 2, "The Meaning of Consciousness."—Ed.]

120 ["Extraversion is characterized by interest in the external object." (*Psychological Types,* CW 6, par. 972) "Introversion, on the other hand, [is] directed not to the object but to the subject." (Ibid., par. 976)—Ed.]

121 See Neumann, *The Origins and History of Consciousness,* chap. 3.

122 "Concerning Rebirth," *The Archetypes and the Collective Unconscious,* CW 9i, par. 217.

123 Rundle Clark, *Myth and Symbol,* pp. 220f.

124 Ibid., pp. 181f.

125 Merrill F. Unger and William White, eds. *Nelson's Expository Dictionary of the Old Testament,* p. 301.

126 *Psychology and Religion,* CW 11, par. 574; see also par. 573.

127 [See Psalm 2:9.—Ed.]

128 *Sartor Resartus,* Book 2, chap. 9, pp. 143ff.

129 *Thus Spake Zarathustra,* part 4, chap. 19, sections 10, 11, in Walter Kaufmann, ed., *The Portable Nietzsche,* pp. 435f.

130 *Memories, Dreams, Reflections,* p. 297.

131 Ibid., p. 359.

Bibliography

Adler, Gerhard. "Aspects of Jung's Personality and Work." In *Psychological Perspectives,* Spring 1975.

Auden, W.H., and Pearson, Norman Holmes, eds. *Poets of the English Language.* New York: Viking Press, 1950.

Augustine, Saint. *Expositions on the Book of Psalms.* In Philip Schaff, ed., *Nicene and Post-Nicene Fathers of the Christian Church,* vol. 8. Grand Rapids, MI: Wm. B. Eerdmans Publishing Company, 1979.

Beer, Rüdiger Robert, ed. *Unicorn: Myth and Reality.* Trans. Charles M. Stern. New York: Van Nostrand Reinhold Company, 1977.

Benet, William Rose, ed. *The Reader's Encyclopedia.* New York: Thomas Y. Crowell Co., Inc., 1965.

The Book of Psalms. London, UK: Cresset Press, 1989.

Carlyle, Thomas. *Sartor Resartus.* London: Everyman's Library, Dent and Sons, 1948.

Charbonneau-Lassay, Louis. *The Bestiary of Christ.* Trans. and ed. D.M. Dooling. New York: Viking Penguin, 1992.

Clark, R.T. Rundle. *Myth and Symbol in Ancient Egypt.* London: Thames and Hudson, 1978.

de Vries, Ad. *Dictionary of Symbols and Imagery.* Amsterdam: North-Holland Publishing Company, 1974.

Douay Bible. New York, NY: Douay Bible House, 1955.

Edinger, Edward F. *The Aion Lectures: Exploring the Self in Jung's* Aion. Toronto: Inner City Books, 1996.

_____. *Anatomy of the Psyche: Alchemical Symbolism in Psychotherapy.* Peru, IL: Open Court, 1985.

_____. *The Archetype of the Apocalypse: A Jungian Study of the Book of Revelation.* Ed. George R. Elder. Chicago: Open Court, 1999.

_____. *The Bible and the Psyche: Individuation Symbolism in the Old Testament.* Toronto: Inner City Books, 1986.

_____. *The Christian Archetype: A Jungian Commentary on the Life of Christ.* Toronto: Inner City Books, 1987.

_____. *The Creation of Consciousness: Jung's Myth for Modern Man.* Toronto: Inner City Books, 1984.

_____. *Ego and Archetype: Individuation and the Religious Function of the Psyche.* New York: Penguin, 1973.

_____. *Encounter with the Self: A Jungian Commentary on William Blake's* Illustrations of the Book of Job. Toronto: Inner City Books, 1986.

_____. *The Mysterium Lectures: A Journey through Jung's* Mysterium Coniunctionis. Toronto: Inner City Books, 1995.

_____. *The New God-Image: A Study of Jung's Key Letters Concerning the Evolution of the Western God-Image.* Ed. Dianne D. Cordic and Charles Yates. Wilmette, IL: Chiron Publications, 1996.

_____. *The Psyche in Antiquity, Book Two: Gnosticism and Early Christianity.* Toronto: Inner City Books, 1999.

_____. *Science of the Soul: A Jungian Perspective.* Toronto: Inner City Books, 2002.

_____. *Transformation of the God-Image: An Elucidation of Jung's* Answer to Job. Toronto: Inner City Books, 1994.

Eliot, T.S. "The Waste Land." In *Collected Poems, 1909-1935.* London: Faber and Faber, Ltd., 1951.

Emerson, Ralph Waldo. *Selected Writings.* Ed. William H. Gilman. New York: New American Library (Signet Classics), 1965.

Fitzgerald, Edward, trans. *The Rubaiyat of Omar Khayyam.* Boston: Thomas Y. Crowell and Co., 1896.

Gaer, Joseph. *The Lore of the Old Testament.* New York: Grosset and Dunlap, 1966.

Ginsberg, Louis. *Legends of the Bible.* Philadelphia, PA: Jewish Publication Society, 1956.

Harrison, Jane. *Prolegomena to the Study of Greek Religion.* London: Merlin Press, 1980.

Jerusalem Bible. Garden City, NY: Doubleday and Co., 1966.

Jung, C.G. *The Collected Works* (Bollingen Series XX). 20 vols. Trans. R.F.C. Hull. Ed. H. Read, M. Fordham, G. Adler, Wm. McGuire. Princeton: Princeton University Press, 1953-1979.

_____. *C.G Jung: Word and Image* (Bollingen Series XCVII:2). Ed. Aniela Jaffé. Princeton: Princeton University Press, 1979.

_____. *Dream Analysis: Notes of the Seminar given in 1928-1930* (Bollingen Series XCIX). Ed. William McGuire. Princeton: Princeton University Press, 1984.

_____. *Letters* (Bollingen Series XCV). 2 vols. Ed. Gerhard Adler and Aniela Jaffé. Princeton: Princeton University Press, 1973.

_____. *Memories, Dreams, Reflections.* Ed. Aniela Jaffé. Trans. Richard and Clara Winston. New York: Vintage, 1989.

_____. *Visions.* Ed. Claire Douglas. Princeton: Princeton University Press, 1997.

_____. *The Visions Seminars.* 2 vols. Zurich: Spring Publications, 1976.

Jung, Emma, and von Franz, Marie-Louise. *The Grail Legend.* 2nd ed. Boston: Sigo Press, 1980.

Kaufmann, Walter, ed. *The Portable Nietzsche.* New York: Penguin, 1985.

Knox, Ronald. *The Psalms in Latin and English.* Ed. Hubert Richards. London: Burns & Oates, 1964.

Neumann, Erich. *The Origins and History of Consciousness* (Bollingen Series XLII). Princeton: Princeton University Press, 1970.

Nicolson, Adam. *God's Secretaries: The Making of the King James Bible.* New York: HarperCollins, 2003.

Nordenfalk, Carl, ed. *Celtic and Anglo-Saxon Painting: Book Illumination in the British Isles 600-800.* New York: George Braziller, 1977.

Patai, Raphael. *Gates to the Old City.* New York: Avon Books, 1980.

_____. *The Messiah Texts.* New York: Avon Books, 1979.

Pelikan, Jaroslav. *A History of the Development of Doctrine.* Vol. 1: *The Emergence of the Catholic Tradition, 100-600 A.D.* Chicago: University of Chicago Press, 1971.

Perera, Sylvia Brinton. *Descent to the Goddess: A Way of Initiation for Women.* Toronto: Inner City Books, 1981.

Physiologus. Trans. from the Latin by Michael J. Curley. Austin, TX: University of Texas Press, 1979.

Rasmussen, Knud. *Across Arctic America: Narrative of the Fifth Thule Expedition.* Fairbanks, AK: University of Alaska Press, 1999.

Sharp, Daryl. *Digesting Jung: Food for the Journey.* Toronto: Inner City Books, 2001.

_____. *Jung Lexicon: A Primer of Terms and Concepts.* Toronto: Inner City Books, 1991.

_____. *The Secret Raven: Conflict and Transformation in the Life of Franz Kafka.* Toronto: Inner City Books, 1980.

Spurgeon, C.H. *The Treasury of David.* 3 vols. Grand Rapids, MI: Zondervan Publising House, 1966.

Unger, Merrill F., and White, William, eds. *Nelson's Expository Dictionary of the Old Testament.* Nashville, TN: Thomas Nelson Publishers, 1980.

The Visconti Hours. Ed. Millard Meiss and Edith W. Kirsch. New York: George Braziller, 1972.

von Franz, Marie-Louise, ed. *Aurora Consurgens: A Document Attributed to Thomas Aquinas.* Toronto: Inner City Books, 2000.

Waite, A.E., trans. *The Hermetic Museum: Containing Twenty-Two Most Celebrated Chemical Tracts.* York Beach, ME: Samuel Weiser, Inc., 1991.

Weiser, Artur. *The Psalms: A Commentary.* Trans. Herbert Hartwell. Philadelphia: Westminster Press, 1962.

Wilhelm, Richard, trans. *The I Ching or Book of Changes.* New York: Routledge & Kegan Paul, 1968.

Index

Page nos. in *italic* refer to illustrations

Studies in Jungian Psychology by Jungian Analysts
Quality Paperbacks

Prices and payment in $US (except in Canada, $Cdn)

Risky Business: Environmental Disasters and the Nature Archetype
Stephen J. Foster ISBN 9781894574334. 128 pp. $25

Jung and Yoga: The Psyche-Body Connection
Judith Harris ISBN 9780919123953. 160 pp. $25

The Gambler: Romancing Lady Luck
Billye B. Currie 9781894574198. 128 pp. $25

Conscious Femininity: Interviews with Marion Woodman
Introduction by Marion Woodman ISBN 9780919123595. 160 pp. $25

The Sacred Psyche: A Psychological Approach to the Psalms
Edward F. Edinger ISBN 9781894574099. 160 pp. $25

Eros and Pathos: Shades of Love and Suffering
Aldo Carotenuto ISBN 978 0919123397. 144 pp. $25

Descent to the Goddess: A Way of Initiation for Women
Sylvia Brinton Perera ISBN 9780919123052. 112 pp. $25

Addiction to Perfection: The Still Unravished Bride
Marion Woodman ISBN 9780919123113. 208 pp. $30/$35hc

The Illness That We Are: A Jungian Critique of Christianity
John P. Dourley ISBN 9780919123168. 128 pp. $25

Coming To Age: The Croning Years and Late-Life Transformation
Jane R. Prétat ISBN 9780919123632. 144 pp. $25

Jungian Dream Interpretation: A Handbook of Theory and Practice
James A. Hall, M.D. ISBN 9780919123120. 128 pp. $25

Phallos: Sacred Image of the Masculine
Eugene Monick ISBN 9780919123267. 144 pp. $25

The Sacred Prostitute: Eternal Aspect of the Feminine
Nancy Qualls-Corbett ISBN 9780919123311. 176 pp. $30

The Pregnant Virgin: A Process of Psychological Development
Marion Woodman ISBN 9780919123205. 208 pp. $30pb/$35hc

The Call of Destiny: An Introduction to Carl Jung's Major Works
J. Gary Sparks ISBN 9781738738502. 10 Illustrations. 192pp $28

Studies in Jungian Psychology by Jungian Analysts
Quality Paperbacks

Prices and payment in $US (except in Canada, $Cdn)

Sacred Chaos: God's Shadow and the Dark Self
Francoise O'Kane ISBN 9780919123656. Index. 144pp $25

The Eden Project: In Search of the Magical Other
James Hollis ISBN 9780919123809. Index. 160pp $25

The Cassandra Complex: Living with Disbelief
Laurie L. Schapira ISBN 9780919123359. 20 illustrations. Index. 160pp $25

Hags and heroes: A Feminist Approach to Jungian Therapy with Couples
Polly Young-Eisendrath ISBN 9780919123175. Index. 192pp $28

The Psyche as Sacrament: A Comparative Study of C.G. Jung and Paul Tillich
John P. Dourley ISBN 9780919123069. 128pp $25

Under Saturn's Shadow: The Wounding and Healing of Men
James Hollis ISBN 9780919123649. Index. 144pp $25

Transformation of the God-Image: An Elucidation of Jung's Answer to Job
Edward F. Edinger ISBN 9780919123557. Index. 144pp $25

INNER CITY BOOKS
21 Milroy Crescent
Toronto, ON M1C 4B6
Canada
416-927-0355 www.innercitybooks.net